Classical World Se. ...

DEMOCRACY IN CLASSICAL ATHENS

Christopher Carey

Bristol Classical Press

General Editor: John H. Betts
Series Editor: Michael Gunningham

This impression 2006
First published in 2000 by
Bristol Classical Press
an imprint of
Gerald Duckworth & Co. Ltd.
90-93 Cowcross Street, London EC1M 6BF
Tel: 020 7490 7300
Fax: 020 7490 0080
inquiries@duckworth-publishers.co.uk
www.ducknet.co.uk

A catalogue record for this book is available
from the British Library

ISBN 1 85399 535 5
EAN 9781853995354

Printed and bound in Great Britain by
CPI Antony Rowe, Eastbourne

Cover illustration:
Jurors' ballots, as used in the fourth century BC, courtesy of
American School of Classical Studies at Athens, Agora Excavations.

DEMOCRACY IN CLASSICAL ATHENS

Current and forthcoming titles in the Classical World Series

Contents

Preface

This book comes with a double health warning. First of all, there is no such thing as a transparent presentation of Athenian democracy. The writer brings an array of prejudices which impact in a variety of ways on the presentation. My own prejudices will be visible enough. Secondly, the scale of this book has inevitably meant omissions and compressions which give the illusion of firmness to issues which are elusive, uncertain and contentious. I hope that the basic approach adopted will at least allow my readers to get behind my account. Where possible I have used quotations from ancient texts to allow access to the primary sources; otherwise I have incorporated as many references as I could. I hope that the irritation of massed references will be offset by the autonomy this allows the reader. The sources are self-explanatory, the few exceptions are listed in the *Suggestions for Further Reading* at the end.

My debts to previous scholarship are immense; the most significant (though not the sole) sources are listed in the further reading section. My thanks are due to Michael Gunningham for his invitation to contribute to the series; writing the book has been far more enjoyable for me than reading it can ever be. I also wish to thank Robin Osborne, who read a first draft and generously took the time to make a number of detailed and invaluable comments; weak or pedestrian points will almost invariably coincide with moments when I have ignored his advice. Finally, my thanks are due to the staff at Bristol Classical Press for turning the word-processed text into a neat volume.

C.C.
May 2000

Note to 2001 Edition

In preparing this corrected edition I have taken the opportunity to remove typographical errors (all mine) and adjust some points of detail. The corrections owe much to an in-flight transatlantic reading by Paul Cartledge, for whose careful comments I am profoundly grateful.

July 2001

List of Illustrations

Acknowledgements

My thanks are due to the following for generous permission to reproduce
photographs and illustrations:

Figs. 1 & 2	The Diagram Group
Figs. 3, 5, 6, 7, 9, 10, 11	American School of Classical Studies at Athens: Agora Excavations
Figs. 4 & 8	Greek Ministry of Culture/Agora Museum
Fig. 12	Boston University, Saul S. Weinberg Collection
Figs. 13 & 14	David Swift

Chapter 1
Sources and problems

Defining democracy

The English term 'democracy' is defined by the *Oxford English Dictionary* as 'government by the people'. But there is no single template for democracy. Among the political systems which claim to be democratic there are wide variations both in the degree of direct popular control of different aspects of the political process and in the mechanisms by which this control is exercised.

The Greek word *demokratia*, 'rule/power/control by/of the *demos*', is as broad as the English term. The word *demos* is used with two meanings. It can refer to the population as a whole (English 'people') or it can refer to the majority ('the masses') as distinct from a more privileged group. *Demokratia* is distinguished on the one hand from systems in which power is exercised by a single individual (*basileia* or *tyrannis*, that is, traditional or non-traditional monarchy) and those in which power is confined to an elite group (*aristokratia* or *oligarchia*). Aristotle in the *Politics* (1317b17ff.) observes:

> The following are the features of democracy. That all offices are filled from the whole population. That the mass rules the individual and each individual rules the mass in turn. That the offices are filled by lot, or the ones which do not require experience or skill. That office is not based on a property requirement, or a minimal one. That the same man may not hold any office twice, or only a few times, with few exceptions, apart from those connected with war. That either offices are held for a short duration in all cases or wherever possible. That all from the whole population may serve as jurors on all matters or on most, and on the most important and decisive.... That the Assembly has absolute power while no office has power on any issue or only in very minor ones, or the Council has power on the most important issues (the Council is the most democratic office...). Then again that ideally all receive pay, Assembly, courts, offices, or failing that the offices, the courts, the Council and the main assembly meetings, or those offices which must dine together...

Aristotle is here identifying the essential features of *demokratia*; but not all of these features applied to every constitution that went by the name. Hence the constant stream of alternatives as he allows for different kinds of *demokratia*. Elsewhere in the *Politics* (1291b-92a, 1318b-19a) Aristotle recognises more explicitly different types of *demokratia*, defined according to the occupations of those with citizen rights and the degree of direct popular control. Like 'democracy', *demokratia* is a kind of system, not a specific structure.

In Athens itself *demokratia* was constantly evolving, at varying rates, from the end of the sixth century to the suppression of democracy in 322 BC. Yet the same terminology is used of different phases in the evolution of the Athenian constitution. Herodotus (6.131.1) describes the constitution set up by Cleisthenes at the end of the sixth century BC as *demokratia*. So too (implicitly) does Pindar. In his *Second Pythian* Pindar lists three kinds of political system: aristocracy ('when the wise watch over the city'), *tyrannis*, and thirdly 'when the noisy host, *ho labros stratos*, [watches over the city]'. This reads like a poetic (and contemptuous) paraphrase of the term *demokratia*. At this date (probably the 470s) it is difficult to see any obvious candidate for his disapproval other than Athens. Thucydides (2.37.1, 3.37.1) has Pericles and Cleon among others use the term *demokratia* for the more radical democracy of the late fifth century. And writers like Demosthenes and Aeschines use the same term to describe the system in operation in the fourth century.

So in studying Athenian *demokratia* we are taking aim at a moving target. In practice however the dearth of evidence prevents a detailed study of the functioning of the democracy in the half century after Cleisthenes. The descriptive sections of this study therefore concentrate in particular on the democracy of the second half of the fifth century and that of the fourth century, the periods for which our evidence, though still patchy, is more substantial.

We could in theory identify either of these as the 'purer' form of democracy. Traditionally the period from the middle of the fifth century until 429, when political life in Athens was dominated by Pericles, has been seen as the Athenian Golden Age, not least because the reverence felt for Pericles by the historian Thucydides still exercises a profound, often unconscious, influence on modern scholars. From this perspective the fourth century can be seen as a period of decline. Not surprisingly therefore many modern studies of Athenian democracy end at the close of the fifth century. Alternatively, since the democracy continued to evolve during the fourth century, and since some aspects of the fourth century system clearly reflect lessons learned in the previous century, the fourth-century democracy can be viewed as the natural end result toward which the fifth century democracy was unconsciously striving. Neither approach will suffice. The first view ignores the stability in Athenian internal politics in the fourth century and is influenced as much by the political power and cultural role of Athens in the fifth century as by any aspect of the constitution. The second view ignores the fact that the most significant steps towards political inclusiveness (apart from the introduction of political pay, see p. 28) belong to the fifth century. It also ignores the fact that, despite the continuing evolution, there is a fundamental resemblance between the different phases, both structurally and in terms of ideology. The fifth and fourth centuries must both be kept in view. The price is untidiness, but it is a price worth paying.

Because Athenian democracy came about through a series of evolutionary leaps rather than a single step, and because the democracy continued to evolve in the classical period, an account of Athenian democracy has to combine elements of description and of narrative; it must be part snapshot and part video. For the reader's convenience I have separated out these elements as far as possible. The evolutionary aspect is treated in Chapter 2, which traces the development of Athenian democracy. For the rest of my account I emphasise the underlying tendencies within the operation of the democracy, while trying to indicate the different manifestations in the different phases.

The sources

Although we know more about classical Athens than about any other Greek city of the classical period, our knowledge is still woefully inadequate. I begin with what we lack. Many countries today (though not Britain) have a written constitution to which appeal can be made when disputes arise over demarcation of powers. Two works entitled *Constitution of Athens* survive from the classical period. The earlier (which owes its survival to the fact that it was at some stage erroneously included among the works of the historian, essayist and adventurer Xenophon) is a (typically) fifth-century exercise in paradox, which justifies Athenian democracy on pragmatic grounds from a stand-point of aristocratic disdain for the masses. Its author, probably a sharp young product of the sophistic movement, has long had to suffer the half-affectionate nickname 'the Old Oligarch.' The later tract, by Aristotle or one of his pupils, dates to the 320s and combines a brief history of the evolution of Athenian democracy with a description of the structures and offices of the late fourth-century democracy. Neither is an official written constitution of (say) the American kind. They are literary/technical tracts rather than authoritative state documents.

In most modern democracies legislation of any kind is usually surrounded by a forest of paper. The final text of the law may be preceded by advance drafts for public consultation. The debate preceding the passage of the law is a matter of record. And in the age of mass media the competing political positions are given a wide and repeated airing. This record is supplemented by the numerous autobiographies of retired politicians.

In classical Athens, however, the general level of documentation was (by our standards) meagre. Although writing began to impact on public life in Greece from the late archaic period, and the inscribing of laws was one of the earliest uses of writing, Athens remained an oral society in many respects throughout the classical period, relying on the spoken word in many contexts where we would regard written documentation as inevitable. Even in public life records were limited. Although law once enacted was inscribed on stone, draft copies of legislation (when such drafts became the norm in the fourth century) were intended for information as part of the legislative process; publication was used for immediate practical purposes and not for permanent record. From the late fifth century the Athenians had a central collection of laws; but the texts survived in a legislative vacuum, except for oral tradition. Though inscriptions show that precise minutes were taken of decisions and proposers of decrees at meetings of the Assembly, no permanent record was kept of the course of political debate. When Thucydides speaks of reconstructing debate in the Assembly (1.22.1), he automatically speaks of the oral testimony of those present, not of public records. So the crucial question of the rationale behind particular pieces of legislation remains a matter for informed conjecture, as it often was for the Athenians themselves in later generations.

Other obvious sources of information are also lacking. The practice of publishing Assembly speeches came late, probably not before the fourth century. So we lack the arguments of the proponents of fifth century constitutional change. Memoirs from public figures are likewise scarce. Thucydides, who must have been politically active in the 420s, gives himself only passing mention in his history of the Peloponnesian War, while Xenophon, who has left us an account of part of his career, was never a significant political figure.

Perhaps the greatest silence, as for most periods of human history, is that of the ordinary Athenian. We can deduce much about the attitudes of the mass of Athenians from the way speakers in court or in the Assembly address their audience. Creative literature gives us some plausible impersonations of the ordinary man, for instance in the comic heroes of Aristophanes, or in the peasant farmer who speaks in Orestes' defence in the trial in Euripides' *Orestes*. But the voices we hear are all created by members of the elite. The ordinary Athenian male, like the Athenian female of any class, is silent.

So what do we have?

Inscriptions

From the middle of the fifth century, in the wake of the emergence of the empire and the creation of the full democracy inscriptional documents become plentiful; before 460 they are scarce. Relatively few public inscriptions deal specifically with constitutional issues. However, they provide valuable information about the operation of the democracy. At the most basic level they tell us about the formulae for recording decisions of the people. Sometimes, through the addition of riders to decrees based on amendments to substantive proposals, they give us an insight into the operation of the Assembly. They provide information on the role of public bodies and public officials, sometimes officials unknown from other sources, on matters of finance and public cult, on the operation of subgroups of the democracy such as the demes, and on the relations between the people and their officials. Many decrees, particularly for the fourth century, deal with privileges granted to benefactors of the people and so illuminate not only status distinctions and related rights but also the operation of the rewards and honours which counted for so much in a society much concerned with public honour.

History and biography

Fifth and early fourth century writers (Herodotus, Thucydides and Xenophon) provide information on the evolution and operation of the Athenian democracy. However, none of these is exclusively or even primarily interested in the Athenian constitution or political institutions. Constitutional information is presented infrequently, briefly and in passing. Sometimes these writers are silent on developments we know or can infer from other sources. Thus Thucydides ignores the reforms of Ephialtes in the late 460s entirely, though he covers this period briefly in the first book of his history. He also ignores Cleon's raising of the pay for jurors in the 420s, despite his evident hostility to Cleon, since his focus is on the war and its interaction with Athenian politics, not on internal political developments for their own sake.

For much of the fourth century we are hampered by the loss of major historical narratives. It is particularly unfortunate that we lack the various histories of Athens, beginning with Hellanicus at the end of the fifth century. We have occasional quotations and citations from fourth century historians preserved in later writers. We can also access the works of these writers through later historical texts, but it is often difficult to determine how far a later account is drawing on the actual words of a classical source, and indeed which source is being used. The problem of authority becomes particularly acute in the case of the biographer Plutarch, a Greek from Boeotia writing in the Roman period. Plutarch's *Lives* present us with a great deal of information about key episodes in Athenian politics. Plutarch was a well-read man and he made use of authoritative sources. For instance, his account of ostracism (*Aristides* 7.5-6) is closely based on the fourth century historian Philochorus. But it is often unclear where the sources end and Plutarch begins. His rhetorical, and explicitly moralising, approach to biography leaves the reader unsure how far he has embroidered events for effect or sharpened contrasts for stylistic or other reasons.

Comedy

Of the great names of fifth century comedy only Aristophanes survives in any quantity. Only fragments survive of his rivals' plays. Aristophanes is represented by eleven plays and a substantial number of fragments (preserved as quotations in later sources or on papyrus scraps from lost collections). The complete plays cover the period from the mid-420s through the first two decades of the fourth century. The poets of Old Comedy engaged directly with the political issues of the day and Aristophanes' plays provide a mass of information about the individuals and institutions of Athenian democracy and relations between the people and the politicians. His *Knights*, for instance, includes an account of a meeting of the Council of 500, while *Acharnians*, *Women at the Thesmophoria* and *Assemblywomen* parody Assembly meetings. The fragments of his rivals' work provide additional snippets of information. However, the comedy of the fifth and early fourth centuries presents contemporary Athens through a distorting lens which exaggerates social and political problems. This element of comic distortion means that the evidence of comedy must be approached with caution.

During the fourth century there was a move toward domestic comedy and the result overall is that the comedy of the latter part of the century (again fragmentary, with the partial exception of Menander) is less informative about Athenian democracy than its predecessors.

Tragedy

Athenian tragedy occupies two worlds. With very rare exceptions the plots of the plays were located in the world of the heroes. But the political structures, concerns and experiences of fifth-century Athens find their way into the plays. The earliest text to address the change in the role of the Areopagus under the democratic reforms of Ephialtes in the 460s is the *Eumenides* of Aeschylus, produced in 458. Though the political amalgam which we find in tragedy (for instance, in plays such as the *Suppliant Women* of Aeschylus and Euripides, where we find kings and democratic structures coexisting) is far removed from the political structures of Athens, tragedy on occasion supplements the limited evidence in Herodotus and Thucydides and allows us to hear echoes of fifth-century discussion of the merits and problems of democracy – and ultimately of the arguments used in political debate to pursue and defend constitutional change.

Oratory

Apart from Andocides' speech *On his return* (probably published early in the fourth century), we have no political speech from the fifth century, though we have a small number of courtroom speeches, real and fictitious, from the last decade or so. Not surprisingly (given the political importance of the courts), some of these speeches provide information on aspects of democratic politics. The practice of publishing Assembly speeches arose during the fourth century. Even so, apart from the Assembly speeches of Demosthenes little has survived. However, we also have a substantial number of speeches delivered either at political trials or at trials with a political motive. Since speeches delivered in court or in the Assembly might be revised for publication, there is always some uncertainty whether we are reading exactly what the first audience heard, but since it is unlikely that speeches were completely rewritten for publication, we are probably reasonably close to the original text. As with all sources, these speeches must be viewed with caution. Since they were always written to secure a particular result, in court or Assembly, the speaker may distort events, misrepresent individual careers or audience practices in order to bamboozle, conciliate or on occasion provoke the audience. The only constraint is the speaker's perception of what an audience familiar with the events can be made to believe, and even this constraint is absent when he digresses to deal with the distant past. A speaker is on the whole more likely to tell the truth where facts are presented in passing as background information rather than as part of the main thrust of the argument; but even here caution is needed. The same caution is necessary in dealing with the political speeches of Isocrates, which were more in the nature of pamphlets than publicly delivered speeches.

But not every speech was written for the courts or the Assembly. One important class of oratory was *epideictic* oratory, i.e. oratory of display. Like all Greeks, the Athenians loved oratory and on certain public occasions grandiloquent speeches were delivered. In Athens the most important occasion for this kind of oratory was the public funerals for the war dead which were held at the end of each year during wartime. These funerals like all ritual were as much about group identity as about religion and the praise of Athens in funeral orations provides an insight into collective ideology.

Under 'oratory' I also include the poetic fragments of Solon. In the archaic period, poetry supplemented prose as the language of political debate, and (in an age when prose had no artistic status) was the only means of placing political views on permanent record. Fragments of Solon's political poetry are preserved in the Aristotelian *Constitution of Athens* and elsewhere. They are a useful supplement to our meagre accounts of the late seventh and early sixth centuries; but they are Solon's own version of his achievements. While we may presume that the account will always remain within the bounds of what an audience familiar with the events will accept, this still leaves a lot of room for creative rewriting.

Philosophers

Philosophy in the classical period was never far removed from public affairs. Protagoras (PLATO, *Protagoras* 318e-319a) claimed to teach his students to manage the household and the city more effectively. The dialogues of Plato present individuals prominent in public life engaging in serious debate on philosophical issues. Socrates is presented by Plato as vocal in his criticism of Athenian democracy. In the *Republic* Plato sketches out an imaginary constitution and in the process advances criticisms of different types of political system. Although the work is more interested in ethical issues than in practical politics, Plato can claim to be the father of political philosophy. He returned to the subject of constitutional theory in the *Laws*. Socrates' execution left Plato with a jaundiced view of Athenian democracy. As a source for the operation of Athenian democracy he is unreliable; but the criticisms of democracy in his works, especially *Protagoras*, *Gorgias*, and the *Republic*, contribute to our knowledge of contemporary constitutional debate, as does the defence of the principles underlying democracy placed in the mouth of Protagoras at *Protagoras* 322c-323a. Plato's pupil Aristotle was deeply interested in political structures. He and his pupils compiled a large corpus of accounts of the constitutions of Greek states; the *Constitution of Athens* (*Ath.Pol.*), already mentioned, remains an invaluable source for Athenian political and constitutional history. Aristotle's more general political treatise, *Politics*, draws on Athenian experience in its treatment of democracy. Given Aristotle's love of taxonomy, it also helps us more than any other ancient text to identify what for contemporary observers and participants were the essential features of democratic politics. However, though Socrates played a minor part in politics, both Plato and Aristotle (who was not an Athenian citizen) are viewing politics from the margin.

Lexica

Something has already been said about later sources. However, a separate comment is needed on the later lexica, which arose in an age when continuing interest in classical Athens was matched by a narrowing school curriculum and a desire, amid a vast body of literature, to access information in summary form. The lexica present a great deal of detailed information on Athenian political practice, often derived from speeches of the classical period. But even where specific authors are cited, we cannot always be certain that the original has been represented correctly; and where no authority is given we are unsure of the quality of our information.

Archaeology

Archaeological discoveries continue to enhance our understanding of democratic Athens and the evidence derived has supplemented our knowledge of the individual demes. Physical remains tell us much about political space in general in Athens and the history of specific structures: the excavations in the Agora, the administrative and religious heart of the city, and on the Pnyx, where the Assembly met, are particularly important. They can be used to check, and in turn can be checked by, the guidebook to Greece written during the Roman period by the traveller Pausanias, which incorporates a description of Athens. Pottery finds have increased our knowledge of ostracism (discussed on pp. 72-3) and in the process have also shed light on the operation of political groups in Athens. In the case of the law courts the excavations have supplemented information available from literary sources about the equipment used.

Fig 1 Map of Greece.

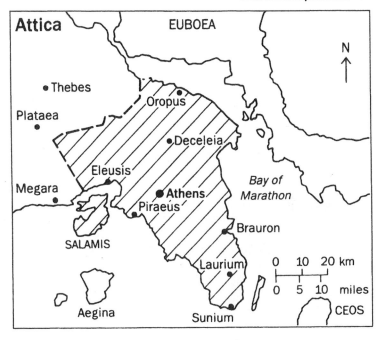

Fig 2 Attica.

Chapter 2
From Aristocracy to Democracy

Radical constitutional change is sometimes brought about by revolution, as in France during the eighteenth century or Iran during the twentieth. In these cases the revolution was ideologically driven; a particular set of political ideas, in the one case secular, in the other religious, played a major role in the thinking of the proponents of revolution and in shaping the new political system. Until the oligarchic regimes at the close of the fifth century, there was no Athenian revolution, in the narrow sense of a single coup which overthrew the previous regime. Democracy came into being by a protracted series of giant leaps interspersed with smaller steps, not in a single bound. There was a democratic ideology in existence by the middle of the fifth century and this certainly helped to shape the radical democracy of the latter part of the century. But the major constitutional changes of the sixth century were driven more by circumstances than by ideology. It is difficult when reviewing the history of the constitution to avoid seeing the radical democracy as the inescapable end result of forces set in motion by Solon. But history is only inevitable in retrospect; different participants, different decisions, could have produced radically different results. To the participants in the various phases it was anything but inevitable that Athens would become a democracy.

Aristocracy in crisis – the seventh century

Our fullest account of the Athenian constitution before Solon comes from *Ath.Pol.* 2-3. The account is condensed and obscure in many aspects of chronology; but it allows us at least to grasp the essential features of the political system. During the seventh century Athens was ruled by an aristocracy. The chief officials, as they were to remain until the fifth century, were the archons, who were selected on the basis of wealth and birth. Their duties included jurisdiction in legal matters. From the account of Solon's reforms in *Ath.Pol.* 7.3 we can be fairly confident that there was already a popular Assembly (*ekklesia*) in the seventh century, though before Solon it excluded the lowest economic group, the *thetes*. It appears to have had little if any formal political power; possibly it functioned as a sounding board for competing views and an arena for aristocratic competition in the manner of the mass *agora* in the Homeric epics. We have no idea how often or under what circumstances it met. The most significant political force in the state was the Council of the Areopagus, which consisted of ex-archons. Its members held office for life. Its powers included oversight over the laws; it was this body which debated issues of constitution and public policy and which appointed the magistrates (*Ath.Pol.* 3.6, 8.2).

But in Athens, as elsewhere in Greece in the seventh century, the ruling aristocracy found themselves under pressure for change; and it is at this period that we find the first tyrannies in Greece. The non-Greek word *tyrannis* was used by the Greeks to designate non-traditional monarchies, in contrast to *basileia*, 'kingship', the term used for hereditary monarchies. The typical pattern appears to be for a member of the aristocracy to set himself up as dictator, *tyrannos*, by representing himself as champion of the disaffected.

Although tyranny was delayed at Athens until the sixth century, we can discern both evidence for discontent and attempts to stave off radical change with concessions. The term used by the *Ath.Pol.* to describe the constitution at this period is 'oligarchic' and probably political power was confined to a narrow group within the wealthy and well-born. Certainly the first attempt to overthrow the regime came from within the ranks of the wealthy. A further force for change was the rise of hoplite warfare with its use of massed lines of heavy-armed infantry, which placed the burden of warfare on those who could provide their own armour: with responsibility for the safety of the state comes a desire for a say in its functioning. Though we have no direct evidence for pressure from this source, the presence of more general disaffection with the existing regime can be inferred from Solon's opening of public office beyond the wealthy.

This dissatisfaction may explain changes in the archonship during the seventh century. According to *Ath.Pol.* 3.4 the original three archons were supplemented by the addition of six *thesmothetai* (literally 'lawmakers'). Though the date is uncertain, the increase in the number of archons was in place by the last third of the century (THUCYDIDES 1.126.8). The change may have been intended to limit the capacity for arbitrary exercise of power by individual archons by expanding the board as a whole.

Whatever the reason for this development, pressure for change remained. In the late 630s or 620s an attempt was made to set up a tyranny (THUCYDIDES 1.1.126-7, HERODOTUS 5.71): a wealthy Athenian named Cylon tried to seize the Acropolis and establish himself as tyrant, with the support of his father-in-law, Theagenes, the tyrant of Megara. The attempt was miscalculated. The Athenians rallied together to put down the coup and many of the insurgents were subsequently massacred. Either dissatisfaction was not sufficiently widespread by the last third of the century to commit large numbers of the population to revolutionary change, or Cylon's use of foreign troops created a suspicion that his aim was to make Athens a puppet state of Megara.

If the panic reaction of the massacre of the Cylonians reflects insecurity within the oligarchic regime, those in power still recognised the need for concessions to the disaffected. In 621/0 (*Ath.Pol.* 4.1) Draco was appointed to write down the laws. There is a general tendency in Greece at this period to inscribe the laws, probably in response to the widespread pressure for change. Although it is impossible to determine how many Athenians could read (at any level) at the time, the public inscription of the laws is not only about consultation. There is enormous symbolic importance in the removal of knowledge of the law from a narrow group of magistrates and its location in public space where it becomes available to the whole population. It is unlikely that Draco made any change to the constitution. In fact, it is questionable whether he actually drafted new laws rather than codified existing practice. Later tradition made Draco's code unusually harsh, but this is probably assumption based on the recodification by Solon and on Solon's reputation as the founder of democracy.

Solon's reforms

Draco's code delayed but did not stop the pressure for change, which was compounded by economic crisis. It is not possible to reconstruct the economic situation in any detail from the trenchant account of the *Ath.Pol.* (ch. 2). We are told there that 'the poor' found themselves in debt to larger landholders. Solon's own claim (fr. 36W.5 ff) to have removed the stone markers, *horoi* (a device for indicating that land was mortgaged), from the earth suggests that 'the poor' in question were landowners, however small their holding, not men without property. Given the limited role of coinage in the Greek world at this period, presumably the 'loans' consisted of produce. The ultimate cause for these 'loans' is irrecoverable; but the statement of *Ath.Pol.* that the poor had to work the land of the rich, together with the terminology used of the smallholders, *hektemoroi* ('sixth-part-men') and *pelatai* (used by later writers to translate the Latin *cliens*, 'client'), suggests that the debt was repayable both in labour and in produce. The net effect was to reduce the peasant farmer to something approaching serfdom; hence the use of the language of slavery (the verb *douleuein*, from *doulos*, 'slave') by *Ath.Pol.* to describe their condition. Failure to pay this share left them and their families liable to seizure as slaves; some at least were sold abroad (Solon fr. 36W.8 ff). It is tempting to see here a sudden crisis; but it could be a slow development. It is even possible that the situation described in *Ath.Pol.* was normal and that the crisis reflects not a change in the economic situation but simply growing impatience among the victims. Restrictive regimes are often at their most vulnerable when they accept the need to change, and it is possible that the concessions made in the preceding decades had merely fuelled the existing dissatisfaction.

By 594/3 the hostility to the ruling elite had brought Athens close to civil war. Solon was elected archon and given the task of mediating between the sides. The *Ath.Pol.* 2.2 calls Solon 'the first champion of the *demos*', placing him in the same category as later figures such as Pericles and Cleon; other classical sources echo the depiction of Solon as 'democratic'. It is unlikely, however, that the ruling group (whose policy had been to make the minimum concessions needed to avert revolution) would have accepted him as mediator if he was perceived as committed to their opponents. Nor does Solon present himself as a partisan of the discontented. In the fragments of his poetry Solon is equally ready to criticise both sides and prides himself on steering a middle course:

> To the people [*demos*] I gave as much privilege as suffices
> neither taking from or adding to its honour [*time*].
> And those who had power and were admired for their wealth,
> for them too I contrived that they should have no dishonour.
> I stood casting my strong shield over both,
> and did not allow either side an unjust victory.
>
> (SOLON fr.5)

Nonetheless, Solon's reforms were wide-ranging, even if they fell short of the demands of the more radical proponents of change. The most important economic measure was the *seisachtheia* ('shaking off of burdens') or cancellation of debts, accompanied by a law forbidding debts incurred on the security of the person. This act had enormous political ramifications beyond the immediate conciliation of the impoverished, since it affected the conceptualisation of the native Athenians collectively as a distinct and privileged group.

There were also major changes in the judicial system. Solon codified the law. The *Ath.Pol.* (7.1) states that of Draco's laws only those relating to homicide were retained (the homicide laws alone were still termed 'Draco's laws' in the classical period); but probably there was far more continuity between the codes of Draco and Solon than our sources acknowledge. A major change was the introduction of the *graphe*, the public action, which allowed anyone to bring a prosecution in certain cases, where previously only the alleged victim (in homicide cases, the family) could sue. This afforded the weak a measure of protection against the strong through the justice system. The judicial powers of the magistrates were restricted by the creation of a right of appeal to a court (*Ath.Pol.* 9.1).

There were also major constitutional changes. The middle-ranking public offices were opened up to the top three property classes: the *pentekosiomedimnoi* ('five hundred bushel men', i.e. those whose land could yield five hundred bushels of dry or liquid produce), the *hippeis* ('cavalry') and the *zeugitai* ('yokemen'). From the fact that we hear of no further change in eligibility for the archonship before the admission of the third class, the *zeugitai*, in 457/6 (*Ath.Pol.* 26.2), it is probable (but not certain) that Solon opened the archonship to the top two classes. Though the substitution of economic for birth qualifications for office probably had only limited immediate impact (Athens was not a major trading state at this period and social mobility through new wealth will not have been widespread), the change was of enormous significance in the long term: it introduced flexibility into a closed and fixed political system, allowing access to office to those with wealth derived from trade.

The lowest property class, the *thetes* ('labourers'), was admitted to the Assembly and to the lawcourts (which at this stage may have been the Assembly sitting in a judicial capacity). We are also told (*Ath.Pol.* 8.4, PLUTARCH, *Solon* 19.1) that Solon created a Council of four hundred – one hundred from each of the four Athenian tribes then in existence. If the statement is true, the Council's role was limited, presumably to preparing business for the Assembly, since the Areopagus retained its traditional role as guardian of the laws and the constitution, with powers to supervise and discipline magistrates (*Ath.Pol.* 8.4).

The sixth century tyranny

The fragments of Solon indicate that his compromise solution to the political tensions left groups on both sides of the political divide dissatisfied; and the two decades after Solon's archonship saw a continuation of the political struggle. There were years when no archon was selected, and there was an attempt by one archon, Damasias, to prolong his office into something like a tyranny. The political divisions took on a geographical form, with the population divided into three groups: the 'Plainsmen' (i.e. from the central plain of Attica) under Lycourgus, the 'Coastmen' under the Alcmaeonid Megacles, a descendant of the archon who executed the supporters of Cylon, and 'the men beyond the hills' (from east Attica), led by Peisistratus (*Ath.Pol.* 13, PLUTARCH, *Solon* 2.9.1, HERODOTUS 1.59.3). Peisistratus' own career illustrates the political instability in Athens at this period, for he was first tyrant and then exile twice, as alliances shifted between the political factions, before he finally consolidated his power in 546/5 (*Ath.Pol.* 14-15, HERODOTUS 1.59-64).

Peisistratus appears to have left the Solonian constitution intact. He maintained his power not by any formal consolidation of his authority but by manipulating the selection of the magistrates (Thuc.6.54.5-6), and by forging alliances with powerful families, as we can see from the archon lists for the 520s, where members of Peisistratus' family appear alongside members of the great Athenian families of the period. The term 'tyrant' summons up images of brutal oppression, but the Greek terms *tyrannos* and *tyrannis* merely define an autocracy as non-constitutional in origin. It was only later that the term *tyrannos* came to mean 'tyrant' in our sense. The rule of Peisistratus appears to have been moderate.

Greek tyrannies rarely survived beyond the second generation, and the Athenian sixth-century tyranny is no exception. Peisistratus was succeeded on his death in 528/7 by his son Hippias. Hippias' brother, Hipparchus, was murdered by Harmodius and Aristogeiton in 514 in a debacle which nonetheless earned them a place in Athenian political legend. Thrown onto the defensive, the regime became more oppressive and was finally overthrown in 510 with Spartan aid.

The Peisistratid tyranny could be mistaken for a pause in the evolution of the Athenian constitution. In fact it was a vital part of that evolution. After Peisistratus' second return, the tyranny provided Athens with three decades of political stability. By allowing time for the consolidation of the constitutional arrangements of Solon, it made a return to oligarchy more difficult. It was at this period that Athens gained territory on both sides of the entrance to the Black Sea, thus pointing forward to the imperial role of the fifth century, while the status of Athens as leading city of the Ionian Greeks was established. Within Athens itself, the reorganisation of state festivals, especially the Panathenaea and the City Dionysia, offered a counterweight to the geographical divisions which had inflamed political rivalry and pointed forward to the reforms of the new democracy at the end of the century.

The reforms of Cleisthenes

According to our sources (HERODOTUS 5.66, *Ath.Pol.* 20.1), the next constitutional leap came about not from ideology but from political pragmatism. The fall of the regime was followed by a fresh struggle for power, between Isagoras and the Alcmaeonid Cleisthenes. To counteract Isagoras' power base within the aristocracy, Cleisthenes appealed to the masses for support. *Ath.Pol.* and Herodotus give no hint of an ideological division between the political rivals. They use the language of political faction rather than ideology for the support for Isagoras (*hetaireiai*) and Cleisthenes (*prosetairizesthai*) and represent Cleisthenes as a democrat by need, not by conviction. This picture may be broadly accurate: increasing the power of the masses was a means of gaining the mandate he needed for his reforms. But since Cleisthenes' main political goal appears to have been stability, he would not have given the *demos* a more central role if he had perceived it as a force for instability. This is pragmatism, not cynicism. The support of the demos enabled him to introduce radical reforms during the very year (508/7) when Isagoras' supremacy in terms of traditional sources of power was reflected in his election as archon (*Ath.Pol.* 21.1).

These reforms irrevocably reshaped the political system. At a single stroke Cleisthenes broke two power bases which had sustained the factional struggles after Solon. The four Ionian tribes of Attica, through which the aristocrats had exercised influence, were replaced by ten new tribes. Cleisthenes also loosened the local allegiances which had formed the nucleus of the factions in the period leading up to the tyranny by dividing Attica into three areas, city, inland and coast, and mixing *demoi*, 'demes' (urban districts or rural villages), from all three to form the new tribes. These new tribes were to form the basis for the selection of a number of officials and for the organisation of the citizen army. The subdivisions of the old tribes, the *gene* (aristocratic clans) and the *phratriai* ('brotherhoods') were left in place – they continued to play an important social and religious role throughout the classical period – but the basis of citizenship from now on was the deme, the smallest formal subdivision of the state. Though Solon has been credited on occasion with the invention of the Athenian citizen, Cleisthenes' fundamental redirection of individual loyalty, through the deme, to the city gives him at least as good a claim to this achievement. Cleisthenes also admitted a large number of non-citizens to the demes, and thus to citizen rights (*Ath.Pol.* 21.4, ARISTOTLE, *Politics* 1275b34-7), effectively enfranchising as many free inhabitants of Attica as possible and in the process ensuring maximum support for the new system.

He created a Council of five hundred (fifty from each tribe); it is not clear whether this was a new foundation or (as supposed at *Ath.Pol.* 21.3) a reorganisation of a Solonian Council of four hundred. The powers of the Cleisthenic Council are nowhere spelled out for us; but probably its main (perhaps its sole) role was to prepare business for the Assembly.

Our information on the Assembly under the Cleisthenic system is sketchy. We have a late fifth-century inscription (*IG* i^3 105) restricting the power of the Council and defining certain key powers of the Assembly. The presence of archaic language has been taken to indicate that the inscription in part copies an original enacting the Cleisthenic provisions. Unfortunately, alternative dates for the original are possible. But the use of the term *demokratia* for Athens after Cleisthenes indicates that the Assembly must have had the final say on major issues of public policy. However, the Areopagus, composed of aristocratic ex-archons, still retained its old functions as guardian of the laws and overseer of the public officials.

Two more measures attributed to Cleisthenes deserve mention. A board of ten generals (*strategoi*) was created (*Ath.Pol.* 22.2), one from each of the ten new tribes, though the Polemarchus retained overall command in war. The generals eventually became the most important public officials in the fifth century. The other measure is ostracism, *ostrakismos* ('the potsherd vote'), under which the individual who received the largest number of votes at a specially designated Assembly meeting was exiled for ten years; this is described in greater detail below (see pp. 72-3). If our sources are correct to ascribe the creation of ostracism to Cleisthenes, it remains a puzzle that it was not used until the 480s; but its introduction is consistent with Cleisthenes' overall drive for political cohesion, since it offered a means of averting factional strife by the crude but effective device of decapitating a faction.

The Cleisthenic reforms were cemented in place by heavy-handed intervention by Sparta. In 508/7 the Spartan king Cleomenes invaded Attica in support of Isagoras but was compelled to surrender after being besieged on the Acropolis for two days. The botched intervention deprived the opponents of reform of legitimacy. A second invasion in 506 crumbled away, providing the newly reshaped Athens with its first major success (*Ath.Pol.* 20.3, HERODOTUS 5.69-76).

Ephialtes and his successors

The first few decades of the fifth century saw a steady consolidation of the system put in place by Cleisthenes. In 487/6 selection by lot replaced election of the nine archons (*Ath.Pol.* 22.5). Though the random selection was still made from a pre-elected shortlist, the change was important, since it significantly reduced the prospects for aristocratic control over the outcome. The consolidation of the power of the demos can also be seen in the use of the ostracism in the context of political competition in the same decade.

The next major constitutional change was initiated in 462/1 by a group led by Ephialtes which included the young Pericles (*Ath.Pol.* 25, 27.1, PLUTARCH, *Cimon* 15.2). Previous reforms had left the Areopagus untouched; but as the democracy grew in confidence, the existence of a body with ill-defined powers which was not collectively answerable to the people must have seemed increasingly anomalous. According to Aristotle *Politics* 1304a 17ff. and *Ath.Pol.* 23.1, the influence of the Areopagus had increased in the period after the Persian invasion of 480-79; the statement may be (though it cannot be shown to be) a fourth century invention. At any rate, political charges were brought against individual members of the Areopagus, while the Areopagus as a whole was stripped of its political powers and left with jurisdiction in a number of religious areas, principally homicide trials. Some of its judicial powers were given to the Council, others to the Assembly and the courts. The transfer of functions from the Areopagus to the jury courts signalled a fundamental increase in popular control over the political process. We can still catch echoes of the propaganda used by the democrats to substantiate their case; the statement in *Ath.Pol.* 25.2 that the Areopagus was stripped of its 'extra/additional powers' (*ta epitheta*) seems to reflect a claim that the traditional powers of the Areopagus were not part of its (supposed) original functions.

Scholars have observed that our ignorance of most of the detail makes Ephialtes' revolution seem more peaceful than it probably was. Even so, considering the magnitude of the change, it is remarkable that there was so little violence. Ephialtes himself was assassinated (the murderers were never found) and a group of disaffected aristocrats conspired unsuccessfully with a Spartan force based in Boeotia in 457 (THUCYDIDES 1.107.4), a move prefigured by Isagoras in his struggle against Cleisthenes and repeated half a century later when the oligarchic coup of 411 crumbled. But the threat of invasion was blocked and the fabric of the state held. We have indirect testimony to the anxieties of this period in Aeschylus' *Eumenides* of 458, which enacts in mythical form the creation of the Areopagus as a homicide court. Given its date, the theme was politically loaded. Though scholars are divided on Aeschylus' own position, it is difficult to avoid the conclusion that the references to the danger of civil war in the play are inspired by contemporary fears.

The work of Ephialtes was consolidated by a series of measures. The third property class, the *zeugitai*, were admitted to the archonship in 457/6 (*Ath.Pol.* 26.2). In the same period pay was introduced for public office and for service on juries. The first of these measures reduced the obstacles which deterred men of more moderate means from seeking office; the second was more significant, given the political role of the courts, since it opened up jury service to all classes, while ensuring an adequate supply of jurors for the increased business of the courts in the wake of Ephialtes' reforms.

Democracy, navy and empire

So far I have focused on constitutional developments within Athens. But to understand the advance of democracy we have to locate internal politics in the wider context of the Persian invasions of 490 and 480-79 and their aftermath. For Herodotus (5.78) victory against Persia proved the value of Athenian democracy, and many Athenians must have had their confidence in the post-Cleisthenic system confirmed or inspired by this success. But there was another, still more important, aspect to it. In the 480s the Athenians had embarked on the creation of the most powerful navy in Greece under the influence of Themistocles. In the wake of the defeat of the second Persian invasion of 480-79, the Athenians assumed the leadership of a confederacy, the Delian League, devoted to following up the Greek victory by liberating the Greek cities of Asia Minor (modern Turkey) and the coastal islands from Persian control. By degrees this confederacy was turned into an Athenian empire. It was the navy which brought victory at Salamis, which offered Athens the means to take the offensive against Persia after the war, and on which the city depended for its control over the empire. The fleet was manned by those citizens who could not afford either to maintain a horse or to purchase heavy armour for infantry service. There was a tendency in ancient Greece for political power to reflect military importance. Just as the hoplites who bore the brunt of land warfare from the archaic period onward pressed throughout Greece for admission to power, so as the navy became the basis of Athenian power the poorer citizens pressed for a greater share in the political process. The point is made succinctly by the Old Oligarch:

> First of all I shall say this, that <it seems> right that there [that is, in Athens] <the base> and the poor and the people have the advantage over the noble and the rich, for the following reason. It is the people that row the ships and confer power on the city,

> and the helmsmen, the boatswains, the naval under-officers, the prowmen, and the shipwrights – these are the ones who confer power on the city rather than the hoplites, the noble and the decent. ([XENOPHON] *Ath.Pol.* 1.2)

The connection between democracy and empire went further. As part of the consolidation of power Athens insisted that all capital cases from the cities of the empire be tried in Athens. This increased the role of the mass juries as an arm of government. The need for a large bureaucratic infrastructure to administer the empire greatly expanded the opportunities for office-holding, a source both of income and of political experience.

Equally important were the broader economic benefits of empire. Except for a small number of states which maintained their nominal independence and provided ships to serve alongside the Athenian fleet, the cities of the empire paid an annual tribute. There was also a substantial indirect income from the empire, for instance in terms of duties on the massive amounts of goods now coming into the Peiraeus and the court dues paid by the allies in the wake of the transfer of capital cases to Athens. The income from the empire was not absolutely necessary to sustain pay for office and for jury service, since (as is often pointed out) the system survived the loss of the empire at the end of the fifth century and was even extended. But as well as helping to finance an ambitious building policy, which both reflected Athens' new status and provided a programme of paid public work, the empire augmented the state income from internal sources and created the financial confidence needed for the introduction of state pay on an unprecedented scale.

The intellectual climate

The Athenian democracy cannot be fully understood without reference to the intellectual climate within which it evolved. The sixth and fifth centuries in Greece were a period of rapid intellectual change, beginning with the Ionian physicists in the sixth century and culminating in the fifth with the activity of the sophists, travelling teachers who found in Athens a favourable environment for their courses on language and rhetoric and their speculations on the world. Apart from its (often iconoclastic) content, the teaching of the sophists was fundamentally revolutionary in the sense that they were proposing to teach *arete*, 'virtue', 'excellence'. This agenda was diametrically opposed to the traditional aristocratic claim to exclusive possession of this complex combination of social, moral and intellectual superiority. The idea of formal instruction was also alien to the aristocratic approach, which favoured learning by example from older members of one's social class. The proposition that anybody could in theory acquire *arete* both gave momentum to and was in turn given further momentum by the egalitarian tendency of Athenian democracy.

The new men

There is one last development in the fifth-century democracy to note. This is not a structural change but a change in the political culture. Even under the democracy Athenian political leaders had traditionally been drawn from old families whose wealth was primarily in land. Political activity had been an aristocratic competition sponsored by the demos; but in the last third of the fifth century a new kind of political leader emerged. The aristocrats did not disappear – Alcibiades for instance was descended on his mother's side from the Alcmaeonidae, who had been prominent under the seventh-century regime. In general, however, the most influential political leaders in the late fifth century – Cleon, Hyperbolus and Cleophon – came from a non-landed background. These were still rich men, but their money came from the manufacture (through slave labour) and sale of goods, and the family wealth was of recent origin. The need to manage and retain empire now made financial expertise an important qualification for political influence (Pericles owed his authority in part to his financial ability); and the scale and relative complexity of their money-making activity meant that men from a commercial background were more likely to possess it than those whose income came from land.

These politicians had a distinctive political style. Thucydides in Book 3 of his *History* represents Cleon, the first of this new breed to achieve a position of dominance, as calculatedly adopting the stance of the simple, uneducated man as a means of distancing himself from the elite and undermining the old style politicians. Aristophanes suggests that this ostentatious, bluff simplicity was characteristic of the new men in general:

> Your only weakness is that you read a bit and badly.
> Demagoguery is not the job of an educated man
> these days or one of good character;
> it belongs to the ignorant and the vile.
>
> (*Knights* 190-3)

Their rhetorical style was equally distinctive. Aristophanes characterises Cleon's debating manner as coarse and violent (*Acharnians* 380-1, *Wasps*

1034). The *Ath.Pol.* adds the interesting detail that Cleon was the first politician to shout abuse and hitch up his robe (for vigorous movement) on the rostrum (*Ath.Pol.* 28.3). Though it is difficult to accept the view of *Ath.Pol.* that Cleon's predecessors had been entirely decorous, probably we should accept that the new men brought a new degree of bluntness to the rostrum.

However, the reaction to this development was mixed. The comic poets relentlessly mock the new politicians for their background, representing them as coarse, uneducated and (with typical comic distortion) of servile origin. Some of this reflects an anxiety created by the political and rhetorical style of people like Cleon. But the Athenians maintained a respect for birth and there was evidently some concern at the transfer of political influence to men of obscure origins, even if collectively they were aware that they needed their expertise.

Oligarchic interludes I: The Four Hundred

By the time Aristophanes wrote his first plays in the 420s the radical democracy was firmly in place. Though it had its critics, the constitution had delivered power, prestige and economic benefits, and aristocrats were happy enough to participate in its success. This did not preclude insecurity on the part of the demos. Late fifth-century sources indicate a widespread, though probably intermittent, fear of another tyranny. The following passage from Aristophanes' *Wasps* gives some flavour of the Athenian anxieties:

> Everything's tyranny and conspirators as far as you're concerned,
> whether the accusation's something big or something small,
> though I've not even heard the word tyranny, not for fifty years.
> But now it's much cheaper than dried fish,
> so in fact the term is all around the Agora.
>
> (*Wasps* 488-92)

Though the picture is exaggerated, it is not invented, for it is supported by Thucydides' account of suspicions arising from the mutilation of the Hermae in 415, when the Athenians were as ready to smell tyranny as oligarchy (THUCYDIDES 6.53.3, 6.60.1). Ironically the demos was, at least in part, looking in the wrong direction: the real danger was from oligarchy. The war against Sparta, fought from 431 to 404 with intermissions, was bound to cause some dissatisfaction, since the financial burdens of war fell upon the rich; but since war also offered them opportunities for military and political advancement, as long as it seemed winnable the danger of subversion was limited. The fact that individuals prominent in the oligarchies of the last decade had been active in democratic politics indicates that any ideological reservations about democracy were counter-balanced by a pragmatic recognition of the tangible successes of the radical democracy.

The situation changed after the destruction of the expedition sent by Athens to conquer Syracuse in Sicily in 415-3. As an emergency measure the Athenians elected a board of ten, the *probouloi*, to handle the daily business of the city in place of the Council of Five Hundred. But there were factions within the city who believed that the democracy was incapable of managing the war against Sparta. When widespread revolt broke out among the subject cities of the empire the people were persuaded in 411 to vote the radical democracy out of existence in the mistaken belief, fostered by Alcibiades, that this would induce Persia to transfer its support from Sparta to Athens. The constitutional change was assisted by a climate of fear generated by a number of assassinations. Under the new constitution power would reside with an Assembly of five thousand; pending the selection of the Five Thousand an interim council of Four Hundred would run the state. Political rights were to be based on property (THUCYDIDES 8.65.3, *Ath.Pol.* 29.5), essentially those of hoplite status and above. All pay for office was terminated.

The oligarchy was fundamentally flawed. With no living experience of non-democratic politics in Athens, the revolutionaries had no consistent ideology and were divided from the start between the moderates who favoured a restricted democracy and the extremists who favoured a narrow oligarchy. This slender alliance fractured when the fleet at Samos refused to recognise the Four Hundred. The extremists turned to Sparta for support and were overthrown under the influence of the leading moderate, Theramenes. The Four Hundred were replaced by the Five Thousand. Thucydides (8.97.2) speaks warmly of the constitution at this period (though he had only second-hand knowledge, since he was in exile at the time) but it did not last and was probably intended as no more than an interim measure; democracy was restored in 410.

Oligarchic interludes II: The Thirty

Oligarchy experienced a final spasm after the Athenian surrender to Sparta in 404. One of the conditions of surrender was that all exiles should be recalled. These included Critias, who became the dominant figure in the brutal regime of the Thirty, set up with support from the Spartan commander Lysander. Under the slogan of restoring 'the ancestral constitution' (*patrios politeia*), they reversed the reforms of Ephialtes (*Ath.Pol.* 35.2). But though the regime began with a semblance of moderation, it rapidly degenerated. The mass executions and appropriations of property drove large numbers into exile. Like the earlier oligarchic revolutionaries, the Thirty were divided between the extremists led by Critias and the moderates led by Theramenes, a struggle resolved when Critias had Theramenes executed. A group of exiles returned in 403 and seized Phyle on the borders with Boeotia; they subsequently established themselves in the Peiraeus and defeated the forces of the Thirty in a pitched battle at Munichia.

The fall of the earlier oligarchy had been followed by reprisals against its supporters in the form of limitations on their political rights. As well as formal reprisals, the continuing hostility against the oligarchic sympathisers kept a number of people out of public life through fear (ARISTOPHANES, *Frogs* 688-91). This atmosphere of intimidation played into the hands of the enemies of democracy and provided the Thirty at the outset with a sympathetic following. In 403 however, in a remarkable gesture of combined generosity and pragmatism, an amnesty was declared for crimes committed under the oligarchy. Exceptions were made for those who had killed with their own hands and for the Thirty, the Ten who briefly replaced them after the democratic victory at Munichia, and the Eleven who had run the prisons and supervised executions; even these could avail themselves of the amnesty if they agreed to submit to a formal inspection (*euthyna*) of their conduct in office (*Ath.Pol.* 39.6).

Although attempts were made by fourth century politicians to excite suspicions of oligarchic leanings against their opponents, oligarchy had ceased to be practical politics in Athens.

The restored democracy

However, it was not inevitable that the restored democracy would replicate the old model. The Thirty had alienated not only radical democrats but also supporters of a limited democracy or moderate aristocracy. Many of these had played an active role in the struggle against the Thirty and some remained active in politics after 403. An attempt was made by one of these, Phormisius, to limit citizen rights to those who owned land, a measure which (it was claimed at the time) would have disfranchised up to 5,000 Athenians. The proposal was defeated; part of the speech written by the speechwriter Lysias for one of its opponents survives as the thirty-fourth speech in modern editions.

Although full democracy based on participation of all adult males was restored, the Athenians had learned from their experiences. Most importantly, procedures for legislation were now more ponderous. The fifth century position is neatly summed up by a remark in Xenophon's *Memorabilia*:

> Everything is law which the assembled mass approves and enacts indicating what should and should not be done.
>
> (XENOPHON, *Memorabilia* 1.2.42)

The new democracy was more cautious. From now on all new laws were subjected to careful scrutiny by panels of *nomothetai*, 'legislators', set up by the Assembly, with elaborate procedures for public display to ensure thorough scrutiny of proposed legislation. During the fourth century there were procedures to make certain that existing laws were not discarded or replaced without careful examination. A distinction was drawn between *nomos*, 'law', and *psephisma*, 'decree': roughly speaking, decrees were measures either of limited duration or with limited scope, laws were lasting enactments or measures with wider scope; and no decree was to have greater authority than law.

We can detect two aims in this more cautious approach to legislation. The first was to protect the constitution: never again could the political system be changed solely by votes in the Assembly. The second was to guarantee some degree of order for the operation of the legal system. The Athenians undertook a thorough review of the law-code following the fall of the Four Hundred, a task which was not fully completed until after the restoration. In the last decade of the fifth century an archive of laws was created. Although the process was probably motivated in part by the need to expunge the changes to the laws made by the oligarchs, the creation of a consolidated archive and the elaborate legislative procedures under the restored democracy suggest that there was a collective conviction that the legislative process in the latter part of the fifth century created the risk of contradiction and confusion. The attempt to remove or avert contradiction is a recurrent feature in Athenian statutes concerning legislation in the fourth century (AESCHINES 3.38, DEMOSTHENES 20.89, 93, 24.18, 33).

However we should not overstate the changes introduced at the restoration. The *Ath.Pol.* (41.2) rightly notes that the period after 403 showed a steady consolidation of the power of the masses. Some central features of the fifth-century democracy were retained in their entirety. What did not change was the central role of the Assembly in determining state policy. Evidently it was felt that the defeat in the war was not the result of structural flaws in the democracy. The Athenians collectively tended to ascribe errors by the Assembly to bad advice by political figures rather than errors by the demos. This tendency was actively encouraged by politicians, who in their struggle for influence regularly attributed bad policy to malice or corruption on the part of their opponents. The essential wisdom of the demos remained unquestioned. In fact, after the restoration the Athenians took a more radical step than any which had been made in the fifth century by introducing pay for attendance at the Assembly (*Ath.Pol.* 41.3).

The consolidation of the power of the masses was also continued in areas such as the procedures for vetting candidates for office, where the role of the lawcourts was expanded. By the time of the composition of the *Ath.Pol.* in the 320s the process had been taken further; the courts now played an administrative role in allocating important religious (and possibly secular) contracts (*Ath.Pol.* 49.3).

At the same time, somewhat surprisingly, the Areopagus experienced a revival. The Areopagus had lost most of its powers under the reforms of the Ephialtes and for the rest of the fifth century it is characterised by silence; but under the revision of the laws in 403/2 the Areopagus was given the role of ensuring that the magistrates complied with the laws (ANDOCIDES 1.84). This was a watching brief only, without significant punitive powers; and sixty years later it still had the power to impose only minor fines ([Demosthenes] 59.80). From the mid-fourth century, however, we can see a gradual increase in its powers. Its responsibility in the area of religion was enhanced when it was given a role in supervising sanctuaries (Harding 78). In the 340s the Areopagus was given the power to investigate and report on political offences, either on its own initiative or at the instruction of the Assembly, under the procedure known as *apophasis* (DINARCHUS 1.1, 1.50) The Areopagus could give a preliminary verdict but the Assembly determined the final verdict and punishment (DINARCHUS 1.54). The Areopagus played an important role in maintaining public order in the emergency after the defeat at Chaeronea in 338.

The accommodation between the democracy and the central body of the pre-democratic state is at first sight surprising. However, the role it was given immediately after the restoration is consistent with the general desire to hedge the constitution round with safeguards. The move shows astute pragmatism on the part of the demos, since the firm inclusion of the oldest public body in the state within the democratic structures at one stroke gave the Areopagus a reason to support the democracy, and blunted the rhetorical appeal of potential anti-democratic claims to restore the 'ancestral constitution'. Furthermore, although the Thirty had restored the old powers of the Areopagus, their main political ally had been not the Areopagus but the Council of 500. Yet it took another sixty years for the Athenians to give the Areopagus a central role in politics and an emergency for them to allow it any substantial punitive powers. The suspicion that the Areopagus might offer support for a non-democratic coup persisted, as we can see from the law proposed in 337/6 prescribing loss of political rights for any member of the Areopagus who served under a regime which supplanted the democracy (Harding 101); and still in the 320s (DINARCHUS 1.62) it was possible to represent the Areopagus as having oligarchic leanings.

It is worth pausing at this point to note a striking omission in the progressive consolidation of the power of the demos. The final logical change, the admission of the *thetes* to office, was never officially enshrined in law, though their exclusion had become a dead letter by the fourth century (*Ath.Pol.* 7.4). Other odd but insignificant anomalies remained in place as traces of earlier phases in the evolution of the constitution. The Treasurers of Athene continued to be selected from the *pentekosiomedimnoi* (the highest of Solon's property classes) in the 320s as under Solon's constitution (*Ath.Pol.* 47.1), though the old classification system was no longer meaningful in the economic climate of the fourth century and a member of this tax class might be poor enough to have to supplement his farming with paid work. The Athenians were not interested in constitutional neatness for its own sake.

Alexander and after

The restored democracy lasted for eight decades. Although Athens never recovered the power it had enjoyed in the fifth century, the early decades of the fourth saw a remarkable recovery and the city remained a major force in Greek politics. From the middle of the century the Athenians were locked in a struggle with the rising power of Macedon which culminated in the defeat of the Athenian and Theban armies at the battle of Chaeronea in 338. Athens was reduced to a Macedonian vassal. On the death of Alexander in 323 Athens instigated a general Greek revolt against Macedon. The revolt was suppressed and the Athenians were compelled to receive a Macedonian garrison and to impose a property qualification for citizenship, thus ending the full democracy.

Chapter 3

Democracy in action I:

The ideology of democracy; the Athenian citizen

This and the following chapters deal with the functioning of the Athenian democracy. As far as possible they treat the classical period as a single entity, though where necessary divergences between the fifth and the fourth century are noted.

Democratic ideology

Although the democracy underwent changes, the principles on which the system was based remained the same. Classical sources agree in identifying freedom (*eleutheria*) and equality (*to ison*) as the key features of democracy:

> It is clear not just in one particular but in every way that equal right of speech [*isegorie*] is of enormous importance, since the Athenians under the tyranny were superior to none of their neighbours in war but when rid of the tyrants were far the best. This shows that when oppressed they were deliberately slack, since they were toiling for a master, but when they were set free each one of them was eager to achieve for himself.
>
> (HERODOTUS 5.78)

> So first of all they are free, and the city is full of freedom and free speech [*parrhesia*] and there is licence [*exousia*] within it for a man to do as he likes.　　　　(PLATO, *Republic* 557B)

> The basis of the democratic constitution is freedom [*eleutheria*] .... One aspect of freedom is that all the citizens shall rule and be ruled in turn. For in fact justice under a democracy is equality according to number, not according to merit, and since this is the definition of justice, inevitably the mass is sovereign and whatever they decide must prevail and must count as justice.... So in a democracy the poor have more authority than the

well-to-do, because they constitute a majority.... Another aspect
is that a man lives as he pleases. For this, they say, is the purpose
of freedom, since it is characteristic of a slave not to live as he
pleases.   (ARISTOTLE, *Politics* 1317a40 ff)

In the first place rule of the mass has the most noble title of all,
equality [*isonomia*].... It holds offices by lot, it keeps those in
office subject to audit, and opens all political planning to public
discussion.   (HERODOTUS 3.80.6)

Firstly you started your speech with a false statement, stranger,
in looking for a tyrant here. For the city is not ruled
by one man but is free.
And the people rules by alternating in turn
each year. It does not give wealth
the most but the poor man has an equal share (*ison*).
                        ('Theseus' in EURIPIDES, *Suppliant Women* 403-8)

It is agreed that there are three kinds of constitution in the whole
world, dictatorship [*tyrannis*], oligarchy and democracy, and
dictatorships and oligarchies are governed by the temperament
of those in power, but democratic cities are governed by the
established laws. You are aware, men of Athens, that in a democracy the persons of citizens and the constitution are protected
by the laws, while dictators and oligarchs are protected by
distrust and armed guards.   (AISCHINES 1.4-5)

The most important feature of democratic freedom was the protection of
the person. The Athenian citizen was protected by law from torture, and
could not be executed without trial (except for a small number of crimes
against property, when a perpetrator who confessed would be summarily
put to death). It is one of the recurrent criticisms of the Thirty that they
killed large numbers of citizens without trial. Freedom also has a collective dimension. For Aristotle and Euripides' Theseus it includes the
prevention of the concentration of power in the hands of a single
individual or group. This is achieved by restrictions on length of service
(usually one year) and on repeated tenure. No magistracy could be held
twice (*Ath.Pol.* 62.3), with a few necessary exceptions. Not mentioned in
our sources as a particular hallmark of democracy, but equally important,
is the use of boards of magistrates, which had the effect of diluting the
power of any individual member. For Aristotle and Euripides' Theseus

freedom includes the subordination of officials to control by the people.

A prominent feature of democratic freedom in our sources is the right of all citizens to live their lives as they see fit: the degree to which Athens in reality recognised individual freedom is hotly contested. The laws placed restrictions (for instance in the areas of inheritance or sexual activity) and made demands on the individual (such as military service); but most of the restrictions on individual freedom related to the protection of *polis* or family or to activities which harmed others. Subject to compliance with the laws, the individual was protected against the arbitrary exercise of power by officials. It is difficult to draw comparisons with non-democratic constitutions, since we are poorly informed about specific Greek states. But it seems that the level of official intrusion in citizens' lives varied and that democracy was least prone to interfere (ARISTOTLE, *Politics* 1322b37-23a7, 1319b28-33). If we may trust our sources (ISOKRATES 7.37, 46, *Ath.Pol.* 3.6), before the reforms of Ephialtes the Areopagus acted not only as guardian of the laws but also of morals and exercised a high degree of intrusion into what, under the democracy, were private activities.

Included in the freedom of Athenian democracy was the right to behave in ways which advertised disaffection with the system. Admiration for Sparta was widespread among wealthy Athenians, some of whom liked to ape Spartan dress and manners, including wearing their hair long in contrast to the Athenian habit of cutting it short. Naturally, some suspicion attached to such people, especially during the Peloponnesian War, and Aristophanes has his chorus of cavalrymen in *Knights* ask for indulgence for their appearance (*Knights* 578-80) on the ground of their military service to Athens. Suspicion of such behaviour was at its height after the Thirty, who were loyally served by the cavalry, and the speaker of Lysias 16, suspected (probably correctly) of having served under the Thirty, urges his audience not to hold his appearance against him (LYSIAS 16.18-19). But no law ever forbade such flamboyant gestures of respect for Sparta.

The Athenians were equally tolerant of explicit criticism of the democracy. One dimension of 'live as one pleases' was freedom of speech, *parrhesia* (literally 'saying everything'). Euripidean tragedy includes debate on the strengths and weaknesses of democracy. Old Comedy both readily lampooned leading political figures and satirised contemporary political structures and processes such as the courts, so central to the democracy, and the administration of the empire. Socrates was vocal in his objections to what he saw as the weaknesses of the system. Though in the end he paid with his life for his views in one of the less creditable acts of the restored democracy, it was his association with the members of the two oligarchic regimes rather than his criticism of democracy alone which prejudiced the outcome of his trial. His pupil Plato (ironically a champion of censorship) was perfectly free to publish his extensive criticisms of democracy, as in turn was Plato's pupil Aristotle.

The major exception to the tolerance of *parrhesia* was in the sphere of religion. In the late 430s (PLUTARCH, *Pericles* 32.2) a decree was passed on the initiative of Diopeithes allowing prosecution for disbelief in the gods or the teaching of astronomy (with its substitution of material for theological explanations of the world). The statement has been doubted, but there is no compelling reason to reject it. We have evidence for the (politically motivated) prosecution of a number of intellectuals for impiety in the final decades of the fifth century and of Socrates, the most notorious example, at the beginning of the fourth. This restriction too (though obviously open to manipulation) falls into the category of the protection of the polis and reflects a need to remove possible causes of divine anger against the community at large. The prosecutions relate not to privately expressed beliefs but to public practice and teaching.

Equality consists in the right of access to the political process to all citizens without distinction of wealth or birth. This includes the right to hold office or to serve on a jury. Prominent among these rights is the one identified by our sources as *isegoria*, literally 'equal speech': it was open to any citizen not only to attend but also to address the Assembly. Theseus in Euripides' *Suppliant Women* declares proudly:

> This is freedom: Who wishes to offer
> in public good advice he has for the city?
>
> (*Suppliant Women* 438-9)

It also includes equality of protection under and access to the law. Other constitutions could use the language of political equality, *isonomia*: the Thebans in Thucydides (3.62.4) use the term *oligarchia isonomos*, 'egalitarian oligarchy', without irony. But what distinguishes democratic *isonomia* is the scale of the distribution of equality.

Though it is useful for analytical purposes to distinguish the concepts of equality and freedom, the two are intertwined in discussions of democracy and often barely distinguishable.

The limits of equality

The ideology of equality, however, had its limits. Equal access to political activity was never confused with an equal right or an equal ability to perform all tasks. The Athenians like all Greeks believed that judgement comes with maturity, and they always discriminated on grounds of age. For service on a jury or the holding of office the minimum age was 30 (XENOPHON, *Memorabilia* 1.2.35-6, *Ath.Pol.* 4.3; 30.2; 31.1; 63.3). There were other limitations on equality. Aristotle and others associate democracy with the use of selection by lot rather than election. Yet even under the democracy at its most radical some offices, specifically those requiring particular skills or experience, were always filled by election. It is worth noting the definition of equality given by Thucydides' Pericles:

> It bears the name democracy because it is governed not by the few but by the majority. All have equal rights in law in private disputes; but when it comes to prestige, as each man is respected in some activity, he receives more honour in public affairs, not by rotation but on grounds of excellence, nor, with respect to poverty, if a man can do some good for the city, does he find himself prevented because of the obscurity of his station.
>
> (THUCYDIDES 2.37.1)

It is striking that even here, in one of the most idealised presentations of Athenian democratic principles, there is no suggestion that all should expect to contribute to the city in the same way. The vision is of a meritocracy in which individual authority is earned by personal ability, not acquired as an automatic right.

There is another respect in which the Athenians never sought equality. Plato's Socrates makes the following claim at *Republic* 557a:

> Democracy, I think, comes about when the poor are victorious and kill some of the rich [literally 'the others'], exile others, and give the remainder of the population an equal share in political activity and office, and in general offices are filled in democracy by lot.

Democracy did in some cases arise from violent revolution; and attempts could be made, in ancient as in modern times, to sweep away the previous elite. But Plato's generalisation is wildly inaccurate in the context of Athens, the only democracy he had encountered at close quarters. The fact that democracy in Athens came about through a series of evolutionary leaps rather than a single violent coup allowed it to retain and adapt aspects of the previous system. This capacity to evolve, adapt and absorb is an important part of the success and stability of Athenian democracy. In a much quoted statement, *Ath.Pol.* reports the announcement made by the eponymous archon at the beginning of his term:

> And the archon immediately on assuming office first of all announces that all the possessions a man had before the commencement of his service he is to keep and control until the end of his term. (56.2)

It is generally supposed that this pronouncement goes back to the archaic period. It reflects the fear of a redistribution of land, a measure which some of the poor hoped for in Solon's day and which was a common demand in Greece at times of revolution. The pronouncement was a recurring reassurance that Athens was governed by law and that individual property, like the person, was protected. There was no attempt to redistribute wealth from the rich to the poor, a common theme in some modern egalitarian ideologies. The Athenians accepted economic disparity as an inescapable fact of life; though politically radical, Athenian democracy was economically and socially conservative.

Nor was there any attempt to bar the elite from power. Instead the democracy sought to harness traditional features of elite activity for the city as a whole. Since the time of Homer the rich and well-born had engaged in competition for prestige – in war, in athletics and in politics. It was characteristic of the Greek polis to appropriate this competition for its own purposes. The great achievement of Athens was to put elite competition to the service of mass democracy. The benefits for the city as a whole were considerable. The absorption of aristocratic competition into the democratic structures and processes provided an outlet for divisive drives which might otherwise have found expression in violent insurrection. While it offered an incentive for the wealthy to identify their interests with those of the democratic state, it also offered a clear statement of the subordination of the individual to the collective good. And it ensured that some at least of their conspicuous consumption was used for the benefit of the city as a whole.

The most obvious example of this process is in the political sphere, where the rich and influential competed for the favour of the demos. This favour was registered partly in tangible rewards and, no less importantly, in the intangible reward of prestige. Political activity offered the individual a means not only of achieving eminence for himself but also of bequeathing prestige to his family. Another area in which elite competition was put to the service of the democracy was the liturgy system, which is discussed in the next section.

The importance of elite competition for the democratic state is recognised by Demosthenes:

> The equal share of privileges among those who have political power creates unanimity in oligarchic constitutions, but competition in which men of merit engage for the rewards granted by the people guarantees freedom in democracies.
>
> (DEMOSTHENES 20.108)

In other words, the successful democracy divides and controls the elite. This is, however, more than an issue of political calculation. The Athenians collectively retained a respect for wealth and birth; and although the Greeks collectively recognised the danger that wealth could corrupt, they were also aware that poverty too could tempt people to crime.

Citizenship

As with other Greek states, the Athenians guarded the privilege of citizenship jealously. Any non-citizen who exercised citizen rights was liable to prosecution by an action called the *graphe xenias*, literally 'indictment for alienhood', and if convicted the alien was sold into slavery and his or her property was seized and sold.

The qualifications for citizenship changed during the life of the democracy. Until 451/0 a man was eligible to exercise citizen rights, provided that his father was Athenian and his mother was of free birth, irrespective of her race. But in 451/0 Pericles carried a proposal to limit citizenship henceforth to those who could demonstrate Athenian birth on both sides (*Ath.Pol.* 26.4, 42.1, PLUTARCH, *Pericles* 37.3). Although the measure did not affect individuals who had qualified for citizenship under the previous definition from exercising their rights, it had the effect of nullifying marriages between citizens and foreigners and preventing such marriages for the future, since the resultant children would not quality for citizenship, and would be classed as bastards for inheritance purposes and therefore unable to inherit more than a nominal sum from their father's estate (ARISTOPHANES, *Birds* 1649-52). The reasons for Pericles' measure are unclear. One obvious reason which suggests itself is a desire to restrict the economic benefits of democracy and empire; it can be no coincidence that the measure was passed in the decade which saw the introduction of pay for a range of political functions. But given the political importance and the self-confidence of Athens at this period, the measure may have been explicitly designed to convert the native Athenians into a closed and privileged group, a mass elite. By the middle of the fourth century the law prescribed severe penalties (slavery with confiscation of property) for foreigners who contracted or feigned a marriage with an Athenian citizen ([DEMOSTHENES] 59.16), but it is not certain that these were part of the decree of 451/0.

The role of marriage in citizenship is a matter of continuing debate. The *Ath.Pol.* nowhere states explicitly that marriage was a precondition, and our other evidence is ambiguous. However, even if bastards were technically able to claim citizenship, this would be difficult in practice, since there was no formal means for a father to acknowledge an illegitimate child. A father would normally admit his children to the *oikos*, the family unit, at a ceremony ten days after birth, but bastards were not full members of the *oikos*. Though the phratries, as sub-divisions of the old tribes, had lost formal political significance under the Cleisthenic reforms, membership of the phratry is often cited in court as evidence for parentage and indirectly for citizenship; but phratry membership was confined to legitimate male issue. In practice therefore it was difficult to prove parentage without proving legitimacy; so whatever the legal position may have been, there was a positive incentive for bastard sons of two Athenian parents to pass themselves off as legitimate.

The exercise of full citizen rights was confined to adult males; women played no direct role in the public sphere in any area except religion. However, women had an integral part in the transmission of citizenship, as they did in the transmission of property, since (at least from 451/0) only a woman of full Athenian birth could give birth to citizens. Accordingly, the Athenians used the same terminology for males and females of full Athenian birth, *astos/aste* ('townsman', 'townswoman'), *polites/politis* ('man/woman of the *polis*').

Citizenship was based on deme membership, which was transmitted from father to son. An Athenian qualified for citizen rights on reaching the age of eighteen, though for the exercise of some rights there were additional age limits. To obtain citizenship the Athenian was subjected to an examination (*dokimasia*) to test his qualifications. He was presented to his deme, who voted whether he had reached the required age and met the birth qualifications (*Ath.Pol.* 42.1). If the majority of the deme members were satisfied, his name was added to the deme register (*lexiarchikon grammateion*). Anyone rejected on grounds of age could reapply in subsequent years; anyone rejected on grounds of birth could appeal to the courts. If the appeal succeeded, the deme was forced to enrol him; if it was unsuccessful, he was sold into slavery.

It was also possible for non-Athenians to be granted citizenship. But nowhere is the jealousy with which the Athenians guarded the privilege of citizenship more visible than in the area of naturalisation. Citizenship was the top rung of an honours system (which included tax exemptions and the removal of some restrictions on the rights of foreigners) used to reward those outside the citizen body. It was bestowed comparatively rarely; and it had to be earned by conspicuous service to the Athenian people. It was sometimes given to foreign rulers to seal an alliance or to Athenian partisans in other states exiled for their political allegiance. It was granted to non-citizens who served in the fleet at the battle of Arginousae in 406 (ARISTOPHANES, *Frogs* 31-4, 693-4, HELLANICUS, fr.171, DIODORUS 13.97.1) and to the assassins of Phrynichus, one of the leaders of the oligarchs of 411. The inscription rewarding Phrynichus' killers survives (Meiggs-Lewis 85; cf. LYSIAS 13.70-3). Since opportunities for this kind of service were naturally few, in practice most citizenship awards to resident aliens were for economic benefactions, such as the donations in cash and military supplies of the wealthy ex-slave banker Pasion (DEMOSTHENES 45.85). Accordingly (with few exceptions) only rich aliens acquired Athenian citizenship.

The process for naturalisation was designed to create obstacles. In most modern societies the acquisition of citizenship is an administrative matter. In Athens it was a legislative matter; citizenship could only be granted by a vote of the Assembly. Our fullest information concerns the procedure in the mid-fourth century. According to our source ([DE-MOSTHENES] 59.89-91, cf. *IG* ii^2 103), two meetings of the Assembly were required. At the first a citizen put forward a decree proposing citizenship. If there was a majority vote in favour, it had to be confirmed at a subsequent Assembly meeting, at which a quorum of 6,000 was required and the vote was taken by secret ballot to prevent intimidation or corruption. Even after this vote, the grant could be challenged, since the proposer could be prosecuted under the action available against illegal proposals (*graphe paranomon*), either on procedural grounds or because the individual honoured did not deserve the award, and if the prosecution succeeded the award was rescinded. Even once admitted to the citizenship, an alien was barred from serving as one of the nine archons or as priest (DEMOSTHENES 59.92).

The term used for rights enjoyed by the Athenian citizen is *metechein tes politeias*, 'to have share in the constitution/political activity/citizenship', or *metechein tes poleos*, 'to have a share in the *polis*'. These rights are nowhere spelled out for us and it is doubtful that there was ever a formal legal list of them; evidently there was a general consensus on what they were. The gulf between citizens and non-citizens in terms of rights was enormous and was daily re-enacted in a variety of ways. Most obviously, the citizen had a right to attend and address the Assembly, to hold office or to serve on a jury; he could also marry an Athenian woman and own land in Attica. Non-Athenians could rent but not own land or houses, though the right to acquire land (*ges enktesis*) could be granted to aliens as an honour. The citizen was also privileged in the legal system. Full access to the whole range of procedures allowed under the laws was reserved for him; some procedures could not be brought by non-citizens.

Citizens were also privileged in having access to certain state benefits: those with a disability which prevented them from working could apply for a means-tested benefit (subject to an upper property limit of three *mnai*, three thousand drachmas); the dole was one obol (one-sixth of a drachma) per day early in the fourth century (LYSIAS 24) and two obols per day by the date of the composition of *Ath.Pol.* (49.4). During the fourth century the state also handed out non-means-tested festival money (*theorika*, literally 'viewing/attendance money') to citizens; originally the aim seems to have been to allow attendance at the dramatic festivals, but it was also applied to a number of other festivals (effectively granting paid holiday). The state also, from the fifth century onward, undertook to pay for the maintenance of the children of Athenian citizens who were killed in battle (e.g. THUCYDIDES 2.46, ARISTOTLE, *Politics* 1268a8-11, *Ath.Pol.* 24.3), a right which was extended to the children of those who died fighting against the Thirty, as we know from the fragments of Lysias' *Against Theozotides* and a partially preserved inscription (Harding 8A).

Finally, the citizen was privileged in religion. The modern distinction between religious and secular activities cannot be applied rigidly to ancient Greece. In Athens there was no social group, from the family upward, whose activities did not include an element of religious ritual, ranging from purification through to libations and sacrifices. The rites of phratries and demes were exclusive to citizens, and at the level of the state full participation across the range of festivals was a privilege reserved for them, though other groups were not usually precluded from watching.

In some modern societies citizens are legally obliged to vote. There was no formal obligation to become involved in the business of the city. The Athenian state relied heavily on individual initiative. It was for the volunteer (*ho boulomenos*) to address the Assembly. And, in the absence of a police force, for the most part it was up to the individual volunteer to take legal action against crimes affecting the state. But there was no legal obligation for the average citizen to do either.

The public duties of the citizen are often described in our sources as 'obeying orders' (*ta prostetagmena/ta prostattomena poiein*). These responsibilities lay predominantly in the military sphere and all Athenians were liable for service of some kind depending on their financial status. Those who could afford to buy and keep a horse served in the cavalry; those who could afford heavy armour served as hoplites. The rest would serve either as light-armed troops (slingers, archers, javelin throwers), as rowers in the fleet, or as marines (*epibatai*), i.e., heavy-armed soldiers serving on board ship, for which they were equipped at state expense (THUCYDIDES 6.42). In the period after the Athenian defeat at Chaeronea in 338 there was a major innovation in military service with the reorganisation of the *ephebeia*, 'cadetship' (from the Greek *hebe*, 'puberty'). The *ephebeia* was probably an old institution, but as part of a policy of ensuring preparedness for war the institution was formalised. On reaching eighteen the Athenian youth of hoplite status was now required to spend two years in military training, including garrison duty (*Ath.Pol.* 42.3).

Liability for military service ended at the age of 59, when all citizens (or possibly all of hoplite status) could be required to act as public arbitrators for a year, as their last compulsory service for the state. In order to reduce the business of the courts, it was a requirement that most private lawsuits should go to public arbitration. The arbitrator's role was to effect a compromise, or failing that to give a judgement, which was subject to appeal to a court (*Ath.Pol.* 53.2-5). The role was not without its risks, since anyone who was convicted of misconduct as an arbitrator was subject to *atimia*, loss of citizen rights; this risk was real, as we see from the case of Straton in Demosthenes 21. 83-95.

For wealthier citizens there were financial responsibilities in addition. Though there were numerous indirect taxes at Athens, except for resident aliens, who paid a monthly tax (the *metoikion*), classical Athens had no regular direct taxation. There were intermittent property levies (*eisphorai*) imposed on the wealthy in times of war, but for the most part financial contributions from the rich were securely anchored to public service (*leitourgia*, 'liturgy'). Prominent among these was the *trierarchia*. The trierarch was given a warship and tackle by the state and was required to maintain it at sea for a year – though by the late fifth century, as the prolonged war with Sparta took its toll, we find trierarchies divided between two individuals, and during the fourth century the burden became largely a financial contribution divided between boards of those liable. The other kind of liturgy was connected with public festivals and most prominent among this category was the *choregia*. The *choregos* was given responsibility for a chorus either in the dramatic or the dithyrambic competitions (choral performances by men or boys) in the state festivals. This required him to pay their wages and cover costume and incidental costs. A partially preserved speech by Lysias (LYSIAS 21) suggests that in the early fourth century a tragic chorus might cost half a talent (3,000 drachmas), while a dithyrambic chorus (depending on the competition and the age of the chorus) might cost anything up to 5,000 drachmas (though this figure includes the tripod dedicated for the victory), at a time when the average daily wage for a labourer was probably about one drachma. The figure given there for service as trierarch (together with LYSIAS 19.42, 32.26) suggests that the full cost of a year's trierarchy might be in the region of fifty *mnai* (5,000 drachmas). Not all liturgies were as burdensome as the *choregia*. But it has been estimated that the total number of liturgies (excluding the *trierarchia*) was at least 97, rising to at least 118 every fourth year when the Great Panathenaea (distinguished from the annual Panathenaea by additional pomp and athletic competitions) was celebrated.

Possession of citizen rights was for life; but it was conditional and the entitlement could be lost permanently or temporarily. The term for loss of political rights was *atimia*, literally 'loss of honour/privilege'. Anyone subject to *atimia* was barred from addressing the Council or the Assembly, holding office, serving on a jury or addressing a court in any capacity; he was also barred from the public temples and the Agora (LYSIAS 6.24, AESCHINES 3.176). He could still marry within the citizen group (though his marriage prospects were poor); he retained his property and his right to own land, though since he could not represent himself in law, he had to rely on friends and relatives to protect his person and property. In some respects a man in this position was worse off than a non-citizen, who could at least represent himself in court. Temporary *atimia* was the automatic result of any debt to the state; and if a man died owing money to the state, his sons inherited his *atimia* until the debt was paid in full. Permanent loss of rights was imposed as a penalty for a number of offences which were felt to be incompatible with citizen status. These included failure to serve on a campaign when called up, desertion in battle, and throwing away one's shield, mistreatment of parents, or homosexual prostitution. The first of these reflects the dependence of the state on its citizen militia for its survival, even in the fourth century when the use of mercenary troops was widespread. The severity of the treatment of those guilty of abuse of parents is based in part on the emphasis placed on respect for parents in Greek belief in general and in part on the interest of the state in the protection of the family. The penalty for homosexual prostitution is at first sight surprising in a culture where there was a widespread (though not universal) recognition of homosexual activity as natural. The Athenians themselves could rationalise the law as reflecting a belief that a man who had sold his body would sell anything, and was therefore singularly corruptible (AESCHINES 1.29). However the root of the Athenian attitude may lie in the male military ethos; a man who sold himself had assumed a passive role more compatible with female than with male stereotypes.

Chapter 4
Democracy in action II:
Organs of control

The Council

Technically the Council of 500 (*Boule*) is an *arche*, a board of magistrates, and in principle is no different from the countless small boards which administered Athens; this is reflected in the rules for appointment and vetting. However, the scale, the central role played by the Council in the democratic administration and its close relationship with the Assembly justify its inclusion here. Its importance is reflected in the fact that it heads the account of the magistracies in the description in *Ath.Pol.* (43.2) of the constitution prevailing in the late fourth century. It is also shown in the readiness of prominent politicians to serve in the Council at critical periods, such as Cleon in the mid 420s (ARISTOPHANES, *Knights* 774-6) and Demosthenes in 347/6 (e.g. DEMOSTHENES 19.154, AESCHINES 2.17), during the run-up to the Peace of Philokrates between Athens and Philip of Macedon.

Council members were selected by lot, fifty from each tribe (*Ath.Pol.* 43.2). As with other magistracies, the minimum age for membership was thirty. The selection was based on the demes, the numbers from each deme depending on its size. In addition a further 500 substitutes (*epilachontes*) were selected by lot. Like all public officials, members of the Council were subject to a preliminary scrutiny (*dokimasia*) to test their formal eligibility, and the substitute would take office in place of any member who was rejected. On passing their scrutiny they took an oath, whose most important clauses were that they would serve according to the laws and in the best interests of city and demos (XENOPHON, *Memorabilia* 1.1.18, LYSIAS 31.1, [DEMOSTHENES] 59.4). By the late fourth century members were paid five obols for each day of attendance (*Ath.Pol.* 62.2). There is some evidence that men of property were disproportionately represented in the Council membership, and the rate of pay (below that for a labourer at this period) suggests the same. There was an exception from the general rule barring reselection for the same office; it was possible to serve twice in the Council. The exception reflects the potential difficulty of finding 500 fresh citizens over thirty every year willing to serve – though in fact it is relatively rare to find people serving twice.

The Council met daily, except for annual festivals (*Ath.Pol.* 43.3). Meetings were open to the public, who were separated from the members by a fence, though the Council could meet in secret, if circumstances required (ARISTOPHANES, *Assemblywomen* 442-4, LYSIAS 31.31, AESCHINES 3.125).

A body of 500 is fairly cumbersome, and the Council had an executive committee to handle business between meetings. This committee was formed by giving the representatives of each tribe responsibility in rotation for one-tenth of the year. The title given to the tribal group was Prytaneis and the period of office was called *prytaneia*, anglicised as 'prytany'. The ten *prytaneiai* formed the basis of the administrative year, which functioned alongside the lunar calendar of twelve months which operated for religious and most practical purposes. During their period of office the Prytaneis dined at state expense at a building in the Agora called the Tholos; they had an allowance of one obol per day for food (*Ath.Pol.* 62.2).

A chairman of the Prytaneis was selected by lot (*Ath.Pol.* 44.1). As with almost all offices in Athens, this could be held only once. It lasted for a day and a night, during which he held the city's seal and the keys to the temples and the public records. He had to remain on duty during that period, accompanied by a third of the Prytaneis. They slept in the Tholos, so that there was always a contingent of the Council on duty in case urgent action was needed. That this was more than just a theoretical possibility can be seen from Demosthenes' account of one such emergency (though in this case the incident happened while all the Prytaneis were still present), when the news arrived in 339 that Philip of Macedon had seized Elatea in Phocis and was within an easy march of Attica:

> It was evening, and someone brought the news to the Prytaneis that Elatea had been taken. At this they immediately rose in the middle of their dinner. Some of them drove the shopkeepers out of their booths in the Agora and burned the wicker frames, while others sent for the generals and called a trumpeter. And the city was full of confusion. (DEMOSTHENES 18.169)

The Council as a whole acted as the steering committee for the Assembly. It gave prior consideration to Assembly business and set the agenda for meetings. Only items which had been discussed by the Council could be put to the Assembly vote (*Ath.Pol.* 45.4). The Council placed business before the Assembly in the form of a *probouleuma*, 'preliminary motion'. This could carry a recommendation from the Council proposing a specific decision (often termed by modern scholars a 'closed *probouleuma*'), which the Assembly was free to accept, reject or amend in the light of debate and alternative proposals put forward at the Assembly meeting, or it might be open-ended, simply proposing discussion of an issue without making a firm recommendation (often termed an 'open *probouleuma*'). In its role as steering committee the Council received envoys from foreign states and granted them leave to address the Assembly (AESCHINES 2.58); Athenian envoys to other states reported to the Council on their return (AESCHINES 2.45-6).

The Council also acted in many respects as the executive arm of the Assembly: it published its own decrees (these begin: *edoxe tei boulei*, 'the Council resolved'), which generally deal with routine matters or with specific decisions devolved to it by the Assembly. In carrying out specific activities on the instructions of the Assembly it was no different from any other board of magistrates. It was its routine functions (some of which were carried out by sub-committees) which made it the Assembly's representative. The *Ath.Pol.* sums up the Council's role (47.1, 49.5) with the words: 'it also co-operates in most of the activities of the other magistracies'.

Foremost among these functions was finance. The multiple sources of income and the large number of officials handling public money meant that direct supervision by the Assembly was never a realistic possibility. This supervision was devolved to the Council.

The Athenian state possessed substantial amounts of property and revenue-generating activities. The Athenians preferred not to run these activities directly in the manner of modern state-owned industries and bureaucracies but to put them out to contract. The silver mines under the soil, even under private land, were the property of the state. The right to work these mines for a specified period was auctioned by officials called the 'Sellers' (*poletai*): it was the Council that voted on the bids (*Ath.Pol.* 47.2). A similar process applied to the right to collect the two per cent tax on imports and exports, the right to collect the monthly metic tax (*metoikion*), and the right to collect the state tax on prostitutes; these concessions were farmed out to the highest bidder (ANDOCIDES 1.133-6, [DEMOSTHENES] 59.27, *Ath.Pol.* 47.2, Harpocration's entry under *metoikion*, AESCHINES 1.119), whose profit was the difference between the amount paid to the state and the tax collected. The sacred land attached to public shrines was leased out by the King-Archon, the *Basileus* (see p. 62 below) in the presence of the Council (*Ath.Pol.* 47.4). It also supervised the sale of private property confiscated by the state from those convicted of intentional homicide and political crimes (*Ath.Pol.* 47.2, 3).

The Council also had overall responsibility for the receipt of money due to the state. The successful bidders for leases and taxes paid either in a lump sum in the ninth prytany or in instalments. The Council, together with officials known as the 'Receivers' (*apodektai*) took receipt of these payments (*Ath.Pol.* 47.3, 48.1). In the fifth century it was the Council which received the tribute from the cities of the empire (Meiggs-Lewis 46).

Its financial role included general supervision of the expenditure of officials. During the fifth century payments from the public treasury were made as needed by the *Kolakretai*, who were supervised by the Council; this role disappeared in the fourth century, when the various boards received their own budgets under an annual distribution (*merismos*). The Council appointed a sub-committee (*logistai*, 'auditors') who examined the accounts of magistrates every prytany (*Ath.Pol.* 48.3; a separate board of *logistai* vetted magistrates' accounts on expiry of office, p. 61). Overseeing of expenditure included supervision of the placing of contracts for public works: by the 320s this task had been passed to the courts (*Ath.Pol.* 49.3), though it seems that the Council continued to supervise projects in progress and maintenance work (*Ath.Pol.* 46.2).

The Council had military responsibilities, primarily in connection with the navy: they were obliged to ensure that a specified number of ships were constructed each year (*Ath.Pol.* 46.1, DEMOSTHENES 22.8).

It also had a judicial role: *Ath.Pol.* (45.2) credits it with judicial authority over other magistrates – this kind of supervision was exercised by the Areopagus before the reforms of Ephialtes. However, the power of the Council was much more limited, since there was appeal to a court against its verdict. The most important aspect of its judicial responsibilities was the receipt of impeachments (*eisangeliai*) for offences against the state. It had powers of arrest, most notably in cases of suspected treason (LYSIAS 13.21-3, DEMOSTHENES 24.63, 144-6), though the oath sworn by its members precluded the imprisonment of a citizen who could provide appropriate guarantees against flight, except in a limited number of cases. Its judicial role included the power to eject any of its own members for misconduct (AESCHINES 1.112).

A number of formal examinations (*dokimasiai*) were also conducted by the Council. These included an annual *dokimasia* of the cavalry (*Ath.Pol.* 49.1). The state invested a substantial amount in the cavalry, since it advanced a loan toward the purchase of the horse (LYSIAS 16.6-7, HARPOCRATION entry under *katastasis*) and also contributed to the fodder. The Council vetted the fitness and the treatment of the horses, the fitness of the cavalrymen and their financial ability to maintain a horse (*Ath.Pol.* 49). The disabled were similarly subjected to an annual *dokimasia* (*Ath.Pol.* 49.4) to ensure that they met the physical and financial conditions for the dole. Both of these functions are connected with the Council's financial responsibilities. The Council also conducted the *dokimasia* of incoming Council members and of the nine archons (*Ath.Pol.* 45.3) and vetted the annual enrolment of new citizens by the demes to ensure that they were old enough (*Ath.Pol.* 42.2).

The Assembly

The standard modern democracy is a representative democracy. Except for referenda, more common in some systems than in others, the population as a whole exercises political control indirectly through individuals or parties which it elects to perform executive and legislative functions for a fixed term. Athens in contrast was a direct democracy. Power was exercised by the people regularly, at short intervals, and on specific issues. It had no government in the modern sense. The demos of adult male citizens was the government, and its term of office had no limit.

The two means of popular control were the Assembly and the law-courts. The Assembly (*ekklesia*) was the sovereign body of the state with continuing responsibility for state policy. Though the demos never met as a whole (Athens never had a meeting place which could accommodate them all), the Assembly was conceptualised as the citizen population in session. Athenian authors generally use the term 'the demos' to refer to the Assembly, and inscriptions recording decrees of the Assembly refer to 'the demos', not 'the Assembly' (*ekklesia*): they begin: *edoxe toi demoi*, 'the demos resolved' or *edoxe tei boulei kai toi demoi*, 'the Council and the demos resolved' (where the Assembly ratified a Council recommendation). Foremost among the responsibilities of the Assembly were issues of peace, war and alliance, the elections of officials whose positions called for expertise which precluded the use of the lot, and the continuing oversight of public officials.

In the fifth century it was also the legislative body and laws could be passed by a simple majority vote in the Assembly (XENOPHON, *Memorabilia* 1.2.42). From the time of the restoration in 403 we find a different procedure in place. The chronology and relationship of the various laws on the subject are not entirely clear (DEMOSTHENES 20.89, 93-4, 24.18-23, 33, AESCHINES 3.38-40). But the consistent element is the selection of 'legislators' (*nomothetai*) from among those who had been empanelled for the year as jurors in the courts. The Assembly retained overall control however, in that proposals for new laws or the repeal of existing ones came before the Assembly for discussion in the first instance. It was the Assembly which decided whether *nomothetai* were needed.

In the fourth century the Assembly was required by law to meet four times each prytany. In the fifth century the laws were less prescriptive: we hear of one occasion in 431 when Pericles avoided having an Assembly meeting for forty days (THUCYDIDES 2.22.1), from which it has been inferred that the minimum prescription at that time was one meeting each prytany.

Although any citizen could address the Assembly, this does not mean that any issue could be raised at will. The agenda for discussion was set by the Council (pp. 44-5 above). During the fourth century at least there were specific fixed items of business which dominated part of the agenda. Arrangements in place for the 320s are described at *Ath.Pol.* 43.4-6. The first meeting of each prytany was called the Principal Assembly, *kyria ekklesia*, at which the Assembly voted on the conduct of officials; two other major issues figured on this agenda – food supply and defence. Political impeachments (*eisangeliai*) could also be made. The likelihood of large attendance attracted by the nature of the business at these meetings explains the other regular items on the agenda. Confiscations of property (which would in due course be auctioned) by the state were announced. So too were claims on inheritances and for the hand of heiresses (*epikleroi*), that is females whose father had died leaving no male heir (in such cases Athenian law allowed the nearest male relative to claim her). In the sixth prytany there were additional items on the agenda of the Principal Assembly: a vote was taken whether to hold an ostracism. It was possible also to bring accusations against individuals alleged to have abused the judicial system by bringing false accusations in order to persecute, blackmail or extract dishonest profit (the term for such an individual was *sykophantes*) and against anyone who had made a false promise to the demos. At the second meeting of each prytany, any individual could make formal supplication to appeal for the support of the demos on any public or personal matter. Aeschines (2.15) tells of one such incident: in 348 a number of Athenians were among the captives when Philip of Macedon took Olynthus in the north and their relatives appealed to the Assembly for assistance. The other twenty Assembly meetings per year had no prescribed business beyond the requirement that three of them must allow for discussion of religious matters, three must admit discussion of general secular matters, and three must deal with embassies; these were however minima, not maxima. The account in *Ath.Pol.* cannot be taken to reflect the full list of agenda prescriptions for the whole of the fourth century; we know (from DEMOSTHENES 24.20-23) that for part at least of the fourth century there was a requirement that early in the year one Assembly meeting should review the laws and determine whether any required amendment or repeal.

In addition to the regular meetings, there was scope for extraordinary meetings (*ekklesiai synkletoi*, 'summoned Assemblies') to deal with business which could not wait for the normal cycle. For most of our period the Assembly also acted as a court for political offences under the procedure of *eisangelia* ('impeachment') as well as receiving accusations. Under the *eisangelia* procedure an accusation was lodged before the Council or the Assembly. Since the Council only had limited punitive powers, any serious allegation coming before it would be passed to the courts. For the fifth and the first half of the fourth century the Assembly itself tried *eisangeliai* made before it; these hearings required additional Assembly meetings. But from the middle of the fourth century the *eisangelia* hearings were passed to the courts.

In the absence of hard figures, it is difficult to determine how many Athenians attended meetings. The scale of the auditorium on the Pnyx hill where the Assembly met is of little use as a guide, since this cannot be plotted with confidence over the classical period. During the fifth century the capacity was about 6,000. It has been suggested that the auditorium was increased in size when the Pnyx was reshaped at the end of the century, which would attest at least the expectation of higher attendance figures; but the issue is contentious and the answer depends on a subjective judgement on the location of the speaker's platform in this phase.

A more useful place to start is the quorum for special votes. For all votes dealing with an individual, whether ostracism in the fifth century or (in the fourth century at least) grants of citizenship, there was a quorum of 6,000. So an attendance of 6,000 citizens was always a realistic possibility, especially since in the fourth century at least (when grants of citizenship were more frequent than in the fifth) there must have been several such meetings a year. But the absence of the 6,000 quorum for ordinary meetings indicates that attendance on this scale could not be guaranteed. On the basis of the quorum of 6,000 for certain meetings we can conjecture a minimum regular attendance of about 4,500 on a very conservative estimate and more probably at least 5,000. On this basis the attendance for meetings with a quorum would increase by between 20% and 33%. This is in itself a dramatic increase. Even if we accept that the importance of the subject generated a heightened interest, any lower estimate for ordinary meetings must assume an unrealistic increase for special votes. On any calculation, the Athenians were an unusually politicised population. It is impossible to get a firm figure for the citizen population in the absence of any census during the lifetime of the democracy. The citizen population (that is, the adult male Athenians) varied with the effects of plague (in the late fifth century) and war but is estimated to have been between 20,000 and 30,000 at various times. The fact that up to 6,000 citizens (20-30% of the total) could be expected to attend the Assembly, even for special votes, is remarkable.

However, *Ath.Pol.* suggests that there were problems with attendance and that this was the reason for the introduction of pay for attending the Assembly at the beginning of the fourth century. It would be unwise to take this as evidence for poor attendance in the fifth century. The Peloponnesian War generated significant fluctuations in numbers attending due to military service (THUCYDIDES 8.72.2), but the absence of any known attempt to introduce pay in the fifth century suggests that there was no great anxiety about numbers. The fact that the oligarchic conspirators of 411 had to resort to the trick of holding the Assembly outside the city walls (THUCYDIDES 8.67.2), in order to deter those without heavy armour from attending and create an audience sympathetic to their constitutional proposals, suggests that a large mass attendance could be expected. The introduction of pay may therefore reflect special factors at work immediately after the restoration: the population had been depleted by war, and in particular the deaths of men of military age will have skewed the population to some degree toward the elderly, who would be less mobile and (in the case of those who lived outside the city) therefore less likely to undertake the walk to Athens. Economic hardship arising from the war will have discouraged people from taking time off for politics. But the date of the introduction of pay (shortly after the restoration, at a period marked by a desire to stabilise and protect the constitution) suggests that the brief statement about poor attendance in *Ath.Pol.* oversimplifies. It is likely that the concern was not simply to maintain absolute numbers but to ensure that the Assembly contained a cross-section of the population and that poorer citizens were represented, a matter of inevitable concern after two oligarchic revolutions in a decade. The means of implementation (universal rather than targeted pay) resembles the theoric fund (see p. 39 above) and may reflect a desire to avoid both the administrative complexity and the odium of means-tested payments. However, the increase in the rate of pay during the fourth century (while jury pay remained static at three obols per session) suggests that the concern about attendance persisted. The rate was set by Agyrrius immediately after the restoration at one obol per meeting, a nominal sum; it was raised by Heraclides to two obols, a sum then outbid by Agyrrius, who raised it to three obols, half a drachma (*Ath.Pol.* 41.3); all this happened within the first decade of the fourth century. Although this looks in part like a competition for popular favour, it also seems to indicate that attendance remained, or continued to be perceived as, a problem; and by the time of the composition of the *Ath.Pol.* (62.2) the rate of pay was a drachma for an ordinary meeting and nine obols for a Principal Assembly.

It is difficult to be precise about the composition of the Assembly meetings: hints in speeches made at them are an unreliable guide, given the small number which survive. Modern experience of meetings in any context suggests that the composition will have varied. Arrangements for the Assembly agenda presuppose this, since ten meetings a year were intended to deal with core issues of crucial importance for popular control or essential for the wellbeing of the state. Presumably there was a hard core of fairly regular attenders among those in the city or in the adjacent countryside. For those in the immediate vicinity of the city, attendance was probably easier for people engaged in agriculture, with its irregular demands on time, than for groups such as small shopkeepers reliant on regular trade. Attendance from the more distant parts of Attica will have been both limited and patchy; even for those living within, say, 25 kilometres of the city it will have involved an overnight stay, and anyone living a few kilometres away would still have had a pre-dawn walk of at least an hour. Even so, with only 40 meetings a year, regular attendance was a possibility for those who were seriously committed to taking part. The attractions of visits to the city for buying, selling, curiosity and visits to relatives must have offered those outside Athens an incentive for at least intermittent participation. It has been suggested that moneyed citizens were a significant presence in the Assembly. There is no way of testing this proposition, but we can be reasonably sure that they were never an effective force for reaction, because the Assembly consistently, both in the fifth and fourth centuries, increased the popular control over the various aspects of the political process.

During the fifth century the Prytaneis, the standing committee of the Council, presided over Assembly meetings. For much if not all of the fourth century meetings both of the Council and Assembly were chaired by a body of nine *proedroi* selected on the day of the meeting from within the Council (*Ath.Pol.* 44.2), one from each tribal contingent except the one serving as Prytaneis. The presiding officials were assisted in maintaining order by the Scythian archers (ARISTOPHANES, *Acharnians* 54, PLATO, *Protagoras* 319c), the slave corps who performed a limited range of police functions in Athens.

We can reconstruct the procedures for meetings of the Assembly both from accounts of real meetings and from Aristophanes, who several times (in *Acharnians, Women at the Thesmophoria* and *Assembly-women*) offers parodies of the procedures. Meetings began early; in *Assemblywomen* (20-1) the women, who have disguised themselves as men in order to push through a measure to transfer control of the state to themselves, make their way to the Pnyx at dawn (cf. *Acharnians* 4). In the 420s at least there were measures in place to ensure prompt arrival. The Pnyx was adjacent to the Agora, which as the main shopping area as well as the administrative centre of the city offered a wealth of inducements to loiter. From *Acharnians* (21-2) it seems that a rope smeared with red dye was drawn through the Agora in order to herd people toward the Pnyx and to mark latecomers. During the fourth century, the introduction of pay for attendance at the Assembly made it easier to ensure good timekeeping, since from *Assemblywomen* (380-91) it appears that at least at that period only a fixed number qualified for pay.

The meetings began with a purificatory sacrifice. A pig was slaughtered and its blood sprinkled round the periphery of the Pnyx. Pollution played an important part in Greek belief and the purification ensured that the participants were not contaminated or deliberations put at risk by the presence of anyone who was ritually unclean. The herald then uttered a prayer (DINARCHUS 2.14, AESCHINES 1.23) and a curse (DINARCHUS 2.16, DEMOSTHENES 19.70), which unfortunately is best known from a parody in Aristophanes' *Women at the Thesmophoria* (352-71), but which was evidently directed against any speaker who took bribes, deceived the demos or threatened the constitution or the city.

The proceedings proper began with an invitation from the herald: *Tis agoreuein bouletai*, 'Who wishes to speak?' According to Aeschines (3.4), originally the invitation ran: 'Who wishes to speak of those who are above the age of fifty?' Once the older men had spoken the rest were invited to speak. But this practice had certainly died out by the middle of the fourth century, and possibly much earlier.

Assembly meetings could be very lively. Thucydides' account of the Assembly at which Cleon received the Pylos command in 425 BC gives some idea of just how lively:

> And [Cleon] hinting at Nicias (who was serving as general and whose enemy he was) and taunting him, said that if the generals were men, they would set sail and capture the men on the island, and this is what he would have done if he were in command. And Nicias, because the Athenians were yelling to Cleon for not setting sail right now, if he thought it easy, and because he could

see that Cleon was taunting him, urged him to take whatever
force he saw fit and attempt it, as far as they were concerned.
Cleon initially was willing, while he thought that Nicias was
pretending to offer to give up command, but when he realised
that Nicias was keen to give way to him, he retreated and
declared that not he but Nicias was general.... And they did what
one would expect of the mob; the more Cleon sought to evade
the voyage and retreat from what he had said, the more they
urged on Nicias to hand over the command and shouted to
Cleon to sail.   (THUCYDIDES 4.27.5-28.3)

According to Thucydides, Cleon's bluff was called by the Assembly.
Given the speed with which Cleon took control of the military situation, his
plans for the campaign (based on the military experience of the general
Demosthenes) were presumably already laid and he may have been
manipulating the Assembly (though given his lack of military experience
some nervousness would be natural); but there is no reason to doubt the
broad account of the meeting, which was evidently boisterous. Plato
presents this as a consistent and unhealthy quality of the Assembly:

'Why, when,' I said, 'a large crowd are seated together in assemblies or in court-rooms or theatres or camps or any other mass
public gathering, and with loud uproar express disapproval of
some of the things that are said and done and approve others,
both in excess, with loud clamour and clapping of hands, and
beyond this the rocks and the region round about re-echoing
redouble the din of the criticism and the praise.'
                                              (*Republic* 492b-c)

We should not put too much trust in this account. Although Plato presents
the Assembly as raucous and undisciplined, surviving decrees show that
it could generate sustained and detailed debate. Not infrequently we find
decrees consisting of several segments, in which a substantive motion is
followed by subsidiary proposals which expand or refine the main motion.
A good example is the decree honouring the assassins of Phrynichus
(Meiggs-Lewis 85):

In the archonship of Glaucippus, when Lobon of Kedoi was
secretary. The Council and the demos resolved, when the tribe
Hippothontis was serving as *prytaneis*, Lobon was secretary, Phili-
stides was presiding, and Glaucippus was archon. Erasinides

proposed: That Thrasybulus [of Calydon] be praised because he is a good man toward the Athenian demos and eager to do it whatever good he can...Diocles proposed: That all else be as proposed by the Council, and Thrasybulus should be an Athenian and should enrol himself in any tribe and phratry he wishes...Eudicus proposed: That all else be as proposed by Diocles. But on the issue of the people who took bribes relating to the decree you passed for Apollodorus....

This is not chaos.

The herald asked: 'Who wishes to speak?' And the possibility of contributions from ordinary citizens must have been real enough, given the emphasis on *isegoria* in our sources. Yet the regular speakers were few in number: they were almost always from the upper end of the economic scale. The ordinary Athenians controlled the debate, but they did so collectively, both by heckling and with their vote, not by active participation.

After the debate, the presiding officials would put proposals to the vote. Except for ostracism votes in the fifth century and those on naturalisation, voting in the Assembly was by show of hands (*cheirotonia*). This included both the election and deposing of officials. We have no evidence for precise counts (sometimes confusing in modern parliaments with smaller numbers) and it is generally supposed that a rough count sufficed.

The courts

The other important organ of popular political control was the lawcourts (*dikasteria*), manned by 6,000 jurors (*dikastai*). Commenting on the constitution operating in the 320s, *Ath.Pol.* observes (41.2): 'The demos has made itself master of everything, and it governs everything through decrees and lawcourts, in which the demos has the power.' The political importance of the courts is recognised in the account of Solon, where his introduction of the right of appeal to a court is seen as one of the most democratic of Solon's measures (9.1): 'when the people have control of the vote they gain control of the political system'; the vote in question is that cast in court (*psephos*, secret ballot), not the vote by show of hands in the Assembly (*cheirotonia*). The intimate connection between courts and Assembly under the democracy is acknowledged by speakers addressing the courts, who frequently say 'you decided' or 'you enacted' when referring to executive decisions by the Assembly or legislation, as though the two were identical. How far the two groups, Assembly-goers and jurors, really overlapped in composition is impossible to determine with any degree of confidence. As in the case of the Assembly, scholars have attempted to extract information on social background from the assumptions apparently underlying statements in surviving speeches; but again the evidence is unreliable. What we can say is that the Athenians were confident that the Assembly and juries shared the same ideology; as can be seen from the progressive increase in the involvement of the courts in the political process during the fourth century.

Though the jurors did not sit as a single body but were divided into panels numbering hundreds or thousands, depending on the kind of case, they are treated by contemporary writers as though they were a single organ. Speakers addressing the court tend to ascribe decisions by any other court to the jury in front of them, as in the following example:

> I am informed, judges, that a certain Bacchius, who was con-
> demned to death in your court, and Aristocrates, the man with
> bad eyes, and others of that sort including Conon here were
> comrades as young men and had the name 'Triballians' [the
> name of a wild Thracian tribe].   (DEMOSTHENES 54.39)

Jury service was confined to citizens over the age of thirty. The 6,000 were enrolled for a year at a time and were selected by lot from all who applied. Once selected, they swore an oath (of which the most important clauses were to listen to both sides without fear or favour and to judge according to the laws). Though it has been estimated that the courts may have sat between 175 and 225 days a year, the number of courts needed on any one day, and therefore the likelihood of being selected for service, varied. When pay for jury service was introduced in the fifth century, the rate was set at two obols a day. The pay was raised to three obols by Cleon in the 420s (ARISTOPHANES, *Knights* 50-1, 800). Though inflation drove up general rates of pay in the fourth century, the rate for jury service remained the same: evidently there was no difficulty in getting people to serve. Jurors were not obliged to turn up every day and for many of them jury service may have been seasonal employment or a fallback when other work was not available. Aristophanes in *Wasps* represents the juries as composed primarily of old men. Though he probably exaggerates, no doubt regular attendance was particularly appealing to those who found it difficult to obtain more strenuous or lucrative work. From Aristophanes' *Wasps* (242-4, 303-5) it would appear that in the fifth century jurors were allocated to a single court for the year. This system was open to corruption, and in fact there is evidence for some jury tampering late in the fifth century (*Ath.Pol.* 27.5). During the fourth century elaborate procedures were introduced to make the allocation of jurors to courts unpredictable (ARISTOPHANES, *Assemblywomen* 681-90); these were further refined by the 320s (*Ath.Pol.* 63-5).

Jury service was not an office (*arche*) and accordingly the jurors were, like the Assembly-goers, answerable to nobody – an idea exploited mercilessly in Aristophanes' satirical presentation of the jurors in *Wasps* in 423 as irresponsible old men with delusions of grandeur. The jury panels served as both judge and jury; though each court had an official presiding, his role was to control proceedings, not to advise or direct the jurors. And as representatives of the Athenian demos, their decisions were not subject to appeal.

Since there was in Athens no police force or state prosecution service, the initiative in court as elsewhere lay with the ordinary citizen. The chief division in Athenian law was between public and private cases. Private cases were held to be a matter between the individuals concerned and so only the alleged victim could take action. Public cases were held to concern the state as a whole and prosecution was open to anyone (the Athenians used the term *ho boulomenos*, 'the volunteer').

The courts were used to try cases of alleged political misconduct, such as receipt of bribes or treason. Accusations of this sort played an important role in the process of competition between politicians, who tended to impute malice and criminality to their opponents rather than error. The courts were not confined to high crimes; they were also formally embedded in the normal political process. Proposals in the Assembly could be challenged by a procedure called *graphe paranomon* (indictment for illegality), under which any citizen could prosecute the proposer on the grounds that the proposal was procedurally flawed or that its substance contravened existing legislation. If the measure had not yet been passed, further consideration was suspended while the case was heard; even after the measure had been passed, the proposer remained open to prosecution by *graphe paranomon* for a year. In the event of conviction the measure fell and the proposer was liable to a punishment assessed by the court. Three convictions brought loss of political rights. The earliest trial under this procedure known to us took place in 415 (ANDOCIDES 1.17); though we cannot rule out the possibility that the *graphe paranomon* was introduced under the reforms of Ephialtes, the absence of evidence for earlier cases suggests that it postdates the 420s. In the fifth century *graphe paranomon* could be invoked against both laws and decrees, but the firm distinction between the two after the restoration brought a need for an additional measure. From now on *graphe paranomon* was invoked against decrees, while *graphe nomon me epitedeion theinai* ('indictment for passing a disadvantageous law') was available against proposers of new laws.

The preliminary vetting of public officials (*dokimasia*) also involved the courts, which would hear appeals from those rejected. In the case of the archons (*Ath.Pol.* 55.2) there was an automatic double *dokimasia*, first before the Council and then before a court. The courts also heard appeals from youths rejected by their deme at their *dokimasia* when they applied for admission on reaching the age of eighteen (p. 37 above). At the end of his term of office each official was subject to an examination (*euthynai*) of his conduct. This consisted of two stages, the first devoted to his financial accounts, the second to his general conduct. At the latter stage it was open to anyone to lodge a complaint (*Ath.Pol.* 48.4-5, 54.2, AESCHINES 3.23). Allegations of financial or other misconduct would be tried by the courts.

During the fourth century the use of members of jury panels was extended to include a key role in the legislative process. The *nomothetai* responsible for the vetting of new legislation and amendments to existing law (see pp. 27, 47-8 above) were drawn from the 6,000 who had sworn the jurors' oath. In the case of proposals to scrap laws currently in operation this actually took the form of a trial, with speakers appointed to defend the laws under threat (DEMOSTHENES 20.146, 24.23).

It would be a mistake however to imagine that the political role of the courts was confined to these explicit functions. Above and beyond the overtly and unambiguously political use of the courts, we find politicians using ostensibly non-political cases to harry their rivals. Charges of impiety (of which the trial of Socrates is a good example) appear to have been particularly useful as a means of covert political attack. The opportunities for attack were increased by the possibility of using agents to prosecute political enemies, or of appearing as witness or supporting speaker in court. Politicians could also be attacked indirectly. For instance, we have evidence for the prosecution of intellectuals associated with Pericles for impiety; this looks like an attempt to taint Pericles by association and undermine his popularity. One of the most diverting of the courtroom speeches which survive is the speech *Against Neaera* ([DEMOSTHENES] 59), which was delivered for the prosecution of an ageing prostitute named Neaera. The real target was her lover, the minor politician Stephanus, and again the aim was to taint by association.

Through the succession of political cases coming before them the courts acted as an additional forum for testing the popularity of politicians and policies, as well as deciding on the specific issues which formed the basis of the trials. Since the courts could reverse decisions of the Assembly, through the operation of *graphe paranomon*, and (in the fourth century) through the *graphe nomon me epitedeion theinai*, it could be maintained that the courts were the supreme authority in the state; and in fact this claim is sometimes made by speakers addressing the courts. Yet such statements should be treated with caution. Though speakers might treat them as a single body, the jury panels collectively lacked cohesion and unlike the Assembly had no power of initiative; their role was reactive only.

Chapter 5
Democracy in action III
Politicians and officials

The servants of the demos

In comparison with any modern democracy the Athenian system was very simple. Beyond such obvious areas as ensuring the food supply, the state had no economic policy. The contracting out of activities such as taxation removed the need for a specialised revenue service. The use of the volunteer system for prosecutions meant that there was no need for an extensive network of legal administrators. The law regulated some aspects of the operation of schools but otherwise the state was not involved in formal education; schools were private. But by ancient Greek standards the Athenian state was a highly complicated organisation, and for some fifth century observers the radical democracy was marked by an excess of bureaucracy (ARISTOPHANES, *Frogs* 1084). The Assembly could decree but for the implementation of its decisions it required administrators. To run the daily business of democracy a small army of officials was required, and these effectively acted as the civil service of Athens. However, the parallel is inexact. Civil servants in most modern democracies are, along with the judiciary, the source of continuity. Politicians come and go; and in some systems the most senior public servants come and go with the politicians. However there is always a large number of low to middle ranking, and in some systems senior, civil servants who form the bedrock of the political operation and ensure a continuity of expertise and a transfer of knowledge. It was precisely this concentration of experience that the Athenian system of annual rotation and the rule preventing repetition of service in the same office was designed to avoid.

The number of public officials was much greater in the fifth century than in the fourth, since the empire generated an enormous amount of administrative business. *Ath.Pol.* (24.3) gives a figure of 700 Athenian domestic officials and 700 overseas officials for the middle of the fifth century. The repetition of the same figure suggests that the text has been corrupted in transmission, but unfortunately we cannot be certain which figure is wrong and by how much. The various internal officials listed for the fourth century in *Ath.Pol.* add up to over 300, excluding the Council; and the list is incomplete. Recent research suggests that a figure in advance of 500 is entirely possible; so 700 home officials may not be a wild exaggeration. The *Ath.Pol.* subdivides these officials into those selected by lot and those elected by show of hands in the Assembly.

Officials selected by lot

In Athens the vast majority of public offices were filled by random selection from among those who put themselves forward. The use of lot is regarded by our ancient sources as characteristic of democracy. The lot is the absolute leveller, placing rich and poor on the same footing and removing opportunities to influence the outcome, either through canvassing or through corruption. What is most striking about the use of the lot in Athens is the sheer range of areas where it applied.

We find officials with a supervisory capacity comparable, for instance, with those in modern departments of trading standards, weights and measures, customs and excise. These include the ten *agoranomoi*, 'market officers' (*Ath.Pol.* 51.1), who ensured that the goods on sale were unadulterated and genuine, the ten *metronomoi*, 'measures officers' (*Ath.Pol.* 51.2), who tested weights and measures, the twenty (originally ten) *sitophylakes*, 'grain inspectors' (*Ath.Pol.* 51.3), who prevented overpricing of grain and excessive mark-up on bread and flour, the ten *emporiou epimeletai*, 'trading zone supervisors' (*Ath.Pol.* 51.4), whose duties included ensuring that two-thirds of the grain which came into the port was transferred to the city.

We find officials who carry out the function of sanitary and planning officers: the ten *astynomoi*, 'town officers' (*Ath.Pol.* 50.2-3) had the job of ensuring that maintenance work on private buildings did not cause nuisance or obstruction. Their job included controlling the price of entertainers at symposia and competition for their services, presumably to prevent public order problems from drunken customers. They also had control over the dung collectors who cleared the streets (apart from horse, donkey and dog excrement, such as one would expect to find in the streets, the ancients were in the habit of using alley ways as latrines, and the same word, *laura*, serves for both) and they had responsibility for collecting the bodies of any who died in the streets. Among the officials responsible for public works we find the five *hodopoioi*, 'commissioners for roads' (*Ath.Pol.* 54.1), who controlled a team of slave labourers who maintained the roads.

We also find officials with responsibilities for specific areas of the justice system, such as the five *eisagogeis*, 'introducers', who had the job of admitting and chairing a wide range of legal cases (*Ath.Pol.* 51.2), the Forty, who had responsibility for most private cases (*Ath.Pol.* 53.1-3), and the Eleven, who had charge of prisoners and executions (*Ath.Pol.* 52.1).

Fig 3 Fragment of an inscription recording the sale of the property of Alcibiades' uncle Axiochus after the religious scandals of 415.

Another category is financial officers, such as the ten *poletai*, 'sellers' (*Ath.Pol.* 47.2), who auctioned leases, concessions and confiscated property (pp. 45-6 above); a number of inscriptional records of the *poletai* survive, including the sale of the property of those implicated in the mutilation of the Hermae and the profanation of the Mysteries in 415 (Meiggs-Lewis 79). This category also includes the ten *apodektai*, 'receivers' (*Ath.Pol.* 48.1-2), who received money paid to the state and (in the fourth century) paid it out to the various boards of officials in proportion to their share of the *merismos* (p. 46 above), and the ten *logistai*, 'auditors' and their assistants who vetted the accounts of officials at the end of their term of office. Finally, some religious officials were appointed by lot, such as the two boards of *hieropoioi*, 'commissioners for sacrifices', ten of each (*Ath.Pol.* 54.6-7); one of these boards dealt with sacrifices ordered by oracles, the other primarily with most of the sacrifices at festivals which recurred at four-yearly intervals.

One body of officials selected by lot deserves separate treatment, the nine Archons. These consisted of 6 Thesmothetae, plus the Archon-Basileus or King-archon (in Greek simply *ho basileus*, 'the king'), the Polemarchos and the Eponymous Archon (in Greek simply *ho archon*, 'the archon') who gave his name to the year; in addition there was a secretary to the board. Even in the late fourth century the nine Archons were paid only four obols per day each, from which they had to pay for a herald and a fluteplayer to attend them (*Ath.Pol.* 62.2). The pay cannot have covered the expenses, and so the archonship retained its social exclusivity.

The work of the six Thesmothetae was predominantly legal: they dealt with a range of cases distinguished either by their importance or the need for speed (*Ath.Pol.* 59.1-6), receiving the complaints, handling the preliminary hearings and chairing the resultant trials. The three archons each had their own individual tasks. The Eponymous Archon had responsibility for a number of festivals (*Ath.Pol.* 56.3-5), choosing the playwrights to compete at the Dionysia and assigning each a chorus-producer (*choregos*; see p. 41 above); he received appeals from individuals selected for that role. He presided over a number of legal cases, many involving the family, for which he had a special responsibility (*Ath.Pol.* 56.6-7). The King-Archon's duties were primarily religious (*Ath.Pol.* 57). These included responsibility for the Eleusinian Mysteries. The cases over which he presided also had a religious dimension, including, and especially, homicide trials. The Polemarchos had until the early fifth century been the chief military officer of the state; this role was still reflected under the democracy in his religious duties, which included the games held in honour of the war dead. The principal legal role of the Polemarchos was in relation to cases involving metics, again reflecting his early role as the leader in state contact with aliens.

The duties of the three oldest archonships were demanding, especially since they exercised most of them as individuals, not as members of a board. It was presumably for this reason that each of them was allowed to appoint two assistants (*Ath.Pol.* 56.1). Some of the individuals identified as assistants to the Archons were (or became) active politicians and this system allowed the Archons to draw on additional expertise.

Most of the offices filled by lot involved routine activities; and the system of boards reduced the burden of responsibility on each individual, so people of modest means and ambitions could undertake them. Hence we find Demosthenes (24.112) distinguishing between the rich man undertaking elective tasks such as the role of envoy and 'a poor man, an ordinary citizen with little experience who has served in an allotted office'. The contrast is forced, like all contrasts in the orators, and of course 'rich' and 'poor' are elastic terms; but probably Demosthenes is right to see the division between election and the lot as mirroring both a social divide and a distinction in terms of political experience and ambition. These tasks were not mechanical, however: all carried responsibility, though shared and exercised within firm guidelines. To the modern age of entrenched bureaucracies the use of lot on this scale, combined with the loss of expertise caused by the obligatory annual turnover of personnel, seems a hopelessly inefficient way to get state jobs done. The whole point of this system is diametrically opposite to the modern notion of leaving public business to experts and functionaries. It seeks to disperse power and political experience as widely as possible among the population, not to concentrate it among a small number. Efficiency is not its primary goal.

It is more difficult to judge the effectiveness of the system. The lot was an aspect of the democratic constitution which attracted criticism. Socrates is represented in our ancient sources as critical of the use of the lot for the selection of officials (XENOPHON, *Memorabilia* 1.2.9, ARISTOTLE, *Rhetoric* 1393b3ff.). Presumably like most administrative systems the lot produced its fair share of incompetence; but at least the use of boards meant that the damage done by any one individual was likely to be small. The procedures for examining the conduct of officials on completion of their term of office would act as some deterrent to the dishonest and inept, and there were mechanisms to depose corrupt or incompetent officials. The fact that the use of lot was gradually extended during the life of the democracy, combined with the readiness of the Athenians to use election where the work merited it, indicates that, whatever its ancient critics might say, the Athenians found that on the whole the system worked in practice.

Elected officials

Although the lot was crucial to democratic ideology, the Athenians themselves were aware that it had its limitations. Lot can be used for jobs which require qualities which are reasonably common (such as judgement, integrity, efficiency, common sense); it is less useful for jobs requiring specific skills and experience. The more important the decisions taken, the more risky the reliance on lot. Posts requiring a high degree of expertise were filled by election by show of hands (*cheirotonia*) in the Assembly. Likewise, because of the need for continuity the usual restrictions on reselection did not apply in the case of these posts. Here we are moving into the world of the professional.

The posts emphasised in *Ath.Pol.* (43.1, 61) as belonging to this category are the most obvious ones – the military offices: this applied to all of them. At the top were the ten generals (*strategoi*). In the fifth century they functioned as a board but during the fourth century they were each given specific responsibilities. Each tribal infantry contingent was commanded by a taxiarch (*taxiarchos*) and each tribal cavalry contingent by a phylarch (*phylarchos*, 'tribal commander'). In addition, there were two hipparchs (*hipparchoi*, 'commanders of horse') with overall command of the cavalry, subordinate to the generals.

Given the crucial importance of the water supply in the dry climate of Greece, it is not surprising that the *epimeletes ton krenon*, 'supervisor of the springs', was elected (*Ath.Pol.* 43.1).

The other major area where election plays a significant role is finance. In general, routine financial management was left to the relevant boards under the supervision of the Council, but there were some posts where the scale of the income or expenditure or the importance of the policy decisions involved placed them beyond routine competence. In the fifth century the officials responsible for the accounts of the Athenian empire, the Hellenotamiae ('treasurers of the Greeks'), were probably elected (a plausible, but not inevitable, inference from the presence of politically prominent figures among their number). During the fourth century we find individual financial officials and boards operating in areas where traditionally the Council would have had oversight. The treasurer of the military fund, *tamias ton stratiotikon*, was elected (*Ath.Pol.* 43.1). During the period of military expansion following the creation of the Second Athenian League in 378, this fund received the unspent residue of the sums which the administrative boards received under the *merismos* (p. 46 above). In the 350s, with the emergence of a more cautious foreign policy in the wake of the Social War, which cost Athens the more important members of the League, the annual budgetary surpluses were transferred into the theoric fund (p. 39 above), and the fund was used not only to provide for citizen attendance at festivals but also for major public works, both defensive and civil (AESCHINES 3.25, DEMOSTHENES 3.29). The officials in charge (*hoi epi to theorikon*) were elected (*Ath.Pol.* 43.1). The importance of this board can be seen from the fact that leading political figures were eager to serve on it: Euboulos in the 350s, Demosthenes and Demades in the 330s. By the 320s the treasurer of the military fund and the officials in charge of the theoric fund collaborated with the Council in the allocation of mine leases and contracts for tax-collection (*Ath.Pol.* 47.2). From the mid-330s the politican Lycurgus controlled Athenian finance for a period of twelve years ([PLUTARCH], *Lives of the Ten Orators* 852b, DIODORUS SICULUS 16.88.1). The details of his position remain obscure but his post may have been *ho epi tei dioikesei*, 'official for the administration' (HYPERIDES fr.118).

The secretariat

The officials we have been considering required clerical support. Unfortunately, we are badly informed about the minor functionaries who serviced the boards. The more significant secretarial posts were filled by lot or election, exactly like the boards themselves. For instance, the Council had a 'prytany secretary' (*grammateus kata prytaneian*), who attended Council meetings, took minutes and kept the records. He was originally elected but by the 320s was selected by lot (*Ath.Pol.* 54.3). The Council 'law secretary' (*grammateus epi tous nomous*), who wrote down the texts of legislation coming before the Council, was selected by lot (*Ath.Pol.* 54.4), as was the secretary of the *Thesmothetai* (*Ath.Pol.* 55.1). The secretary who read out the documents to the Council and the Assembly (there were no agenda papers and no drafts of proposals were circulated) was elected (*Ath.Pol.* 54.5). These secretaries might in turn have under-secretaries (Greek *hypogrammateus*) working for them. Less significant posts were filled by professionals or by slaves. The secretary who assisted the Receivers and kept the records of payments due was a slave (*Ath.Pol.* 47.5). In order to limit the influence of the professional secretaries, by the early fourth century it was forbidden for anyone to serve twice as under-secretary to the same board (LYSIAS 30.29). However, this would not prevent a secretary circulating among the boards and we find at least one case (Nicomachus, attacked in LYSIAS 30) of a secretary working his way up to a position of some importance in the redrafting of the laws before and after the restoration.

The secretary would often be the point of contact for anyone doing business with the boards of officials ([DEMOSTHENES] 58.8). Not surprisingly, as is often the case with minor bureaucrats, there appears to have been a strong prejudice against such people. Aristophanes in *Frogs* (1084) has Aeschylus complain that the city is overrun with under-secretaries, and Demosthenes is able to exploit his opponent Aeschines' early career as an under-secretary against him (19.70).

Public speakers

Various terms are used by the Athenians to designate active politicians.

The verb *politeuesthai* means simply 'be a citizen', but those who conspicuously use their right to participate in the city's affairs are described as a class as *hoi politeuomenoi* 'those who are active in politics'. The term *demagogos*, 'leader of the demos' is also used, sometimes (from critics of democracy) with a perceptible air of disapproval (like the modern derivative 'demagogue'), though equally it may have a neutral sense. More common in the latter part of the fifth century is the term *prostates tou demou*, 'champion/protector of the *demos*'. From the late fifth century the term *rhetor*, 'speaker', becomes common as a generic term for politicians. Its frequency reflects the fact that public speech before the Assembly is the way to shape policy under the democracy.

For much of the fifth century the post of general was held by major political figures. People like Pericles owed their credibility with the people in part to their military successes. But during the last third of the century we find a divorce between military and political leadership, with the Assembly dominated by speakers who owe their authority to their oratorical skills and political judgement, not to their military proficiency, though even after Pericles we find figures like Nicias and Alcibiades combining activity in the Assembly with military command. During the fourth century there is an almost complete divorce between military command and public speaking (noted by ARISTOTLE, *Politics* 1305a11ff.). While we still occasionally find people who combine regular intervention in debate with military command (notably Phocion from the middle of the century), the more common pattern was for public speakers to forge alliances with generals. The combination of major elective posts with activity on the Pnyx re-emerges from the middle of the fourth century: the difference being it was now financial, not military, office which was sought. However, in the age of Demosthenes, as in the age of Pericles, the Pnyx was the centre of political power. A brief exchange in Aristophanes' *Peace* neatly sums up the realities of democratic politics. The goddess Peace, newly rescued by the hero Trygaeus from the cave in which she had been imprisoned, asks (through the god Hermes) for news of Athens:

> HERMES: And now hear what next she just asked me:
> who now has control of the stone [i.e. the rostrum] on the Pnyx?
> TRYGAEUS: Hyperbolus is now master of that terrain.
> (ARISTOPHANES, *Peace* 679-81)

We occasionally find individuals who influence politics from behind the scenes, like Antiphon in the fifth century, of whom Thucydides observes:

'he preferred not to appear in the Assembly or in any other public meeting, but though he was distrusted by the mass because of his reputation for cleverness, he was nonetheless more able than anyone else to aid anyone on trial in the courts or in the Assembly who consulted him' (THUCYDIDES 8.68.1). But it is no coincidence that Antiphon was the leading light in the oligarchic coup of 411.

To the modern reader of Thucydides or Xenophon, perhaps the most striking aspect of political debate is the emphasis placed on the individual. This is especially true of the stylised debates in Thucydides, where the competing views are set against each other in the form of matching speeches, creating a verbal contest which is reminiscent of the duel of the Homeric hero. In the absence of political parties (a relatively recent development in democratic systems) it was up to the individual to convince the demos that his policy was the right one. And his popularity was tested repeatedly in successive Assembly meetings. This does not mean that there were no political alliances. We have evidence for groupings of politicians who shared the same view on specific issues, generally clustered round a single dominant figure. Aristophanes gives a vivid portrayal of such a group in his description of his bugbear Cleon (cast in the role of a mythical monster):

From his eyes flashed the most fearsome rays of Cynne [a courtesan], while a hundred heads of cursed flatterers licked about his head, and he had the voice of a death-dealing torrent.
(*Wasps* 1032-4, *Peace* 755-7)

The 'flatterers' here are the members of Cleon's political group. But these associations lacked the cohesion of modern political parties. They were essentially personal alliances; though some were longlasting, at certain times, particularly in the middle of the fourth century when Athens had to face the rising power of Macedon, we find kaleidoscopic shifts of allegiance. Unlike many modern democracies, where the serious competition is between two political parties, at Athens there were usually several groups operating at any one time. For instance, in the middle of the fourth century scholars have identified at least three groups in action: the supporters of peace with Macedon as necessary for Athens' longterm security; the hardliners who opposed any accommodation with Macedon; and those who favoured peace as a temporary measure.

Despite his central role in Athenian politics, the public speaker was never a public official. There is some evidence that limited attempts were made to formalise his role. Although we have no precise evidence for the date of the laws in question, the use of the word *rhetor* as a semi-technical term for a regular speaker in the Assembly points to the late fifth century at the earliest, and the most plausible period is at or after the restoration of 403. One source (DINARCHUS 1.71) claims that the law required *rhetores* to have children and land in Attica, that is, they should have a stake in the country they saw fit to advise. This would place them on a par with generals and phylarchs (*Ath.Pol.* 4.2). However, even if our source is reliable, there is no evidence that the law was applied strictly in practice. More certain is the procedure called *dokimasia rhetoron*, 'scrutiny of public speakers'. Despite its name, this was a kind of legal action: it could be activated by any citizen and involved an accusation that a *rhetor* was barred from addressing the Assembly. Our only surviving example is the case brought by Aeschines against Timarchus in 346, based on an accusation that he had prostituted himself as a young man (AESCHINES 1). Other grounds we know of were mistreatment of parents, military offences, and squandering one's inheritance. The penalty imposed if the jury found for the prosecution was loss of citizen rights (cf. discussion on *atimia*, p. 41 above). The use of the term *dokimasia* assimilates the *rhetor* to state officials (for the *dokmasia* of officials see pp. 47, 57 above). However there is a crucial difference: unlike other *dokimasia* procedures, this was not automatic but had to be initiated by *ho boulomenos*. The role of the *rhetor* is never fully formalised.

There is a very good reason for this. Though the Athenians were aware that the regular speakers in the Assembly made up a minute proportion of the citizen population, it would have undermined the democratic principle of free speech to professionalise this activity. In that respect, modern translations of the term *rhetor* as 'politician', though often inevitable, blur a vital difference. The public speaker was a professional only in the limited sense that he devoted a major proportion of his time to politics. He received no salary from the state. As a result, we rarely find a regular speaker who comes from a genuinely underprivileged background. To dedicate one's time to political activity in such a system requires leisure, and therefore money, either from land or from manufacture and trade. Even the institution of pay for attendance at the Assembly made little difference to this system. An active politician needed free time between Assembly meetings to plan and to negotiate with potential allies. Diodotus, Cleon's opponent in Thucydides' account of the Mytilenaean debate of 427, observes:

> In matters of the greatest importance and on an issue of this
> nature, we must look further ahead when we speak than you who

give matters brief consideration, especially as we are responsible
when we give advice while you bear no responsibility when you
listen to us.   (THUCYDIDES 3.43.4)

The role of litigation in politics meant further that an active politician
also needed sufficient time to be in court as prosecutor, defendant, witness or supporting speaker, as well as money to meet fines if successfully
prosecuted by opponents. Money was also needed to pay agents to prosecute one's political enemies. Though not essential, lavish performance
of liturgies was an invaluable way for the aspiring politician to demonstrate his patriotism. In the fifth century, and even occasionally in the
fourth, this practice was extended beyond the festivals of the polis. We
find men with political ambitions using victories in the great panhellenic
athletic festivals (then, as now, a source of collective pride) as a basis for
public prominence and popularity – an aristocratic practice as old as the
ill-advised Cylon (see pp. 13-14 above), who was an Olympic victor
(THUCYDIDES 1.126). In Thucydides' account of the debate preceding
the Sicilian expedition, Alcibiades exploits his success in the Olympic
chariot-race as a claim to popular respect (6.16.2). All this meant that the
Athenian who had to work his land or hire out his labour had little
prospect of penetrating the circle of influence. With rare exceptions, anyone
wishing to play a continuing role in the Assembly needed to have a substantial income, from large-scale farming or from trade or manufacture.
     Since the *rhetor* had no official position, there could be no formal
apprenticeship. The aspiring politician would attach himself to one of
the existing political groupings and make himself useful in a variety of
ways. The speech *Against Neaera* ([DEMOSTHENES] 59.43) describes the
early career of a minor politician of the mid-fourth century, Stephanus:

> Stephanus here had no income worth mentioning from political
> activity; he was not yet a public speaker but still only a syko-
> phant, the sort who shout by the speaker's platform and hire
> themselves to bring indictments and denunciations and put their
> names to other people's proposals, until he fell under the influ-
> ence of Callistratus of Aphidna.

The speaker is attacking an enemy; so the route to influence is presented
in the worst possible light. But the picture of the minor politician as a
member of a claque in the Assembly (intended to exaggerate the support
for a given speaker and so influence the voting), as a front man for
proposals in the Assembly, and as a prosecutor used against political

opponents of a faction or its leader, is both plausible and consistent with what we learn from other sources. Especially noteworthy here is the reference to prosecutions. In Athens, as in republican Rome, one way for the aspiring politician to achieve notoriety was to prosecute prominent figures. Pericles early in his career prosecuted Cimon, the leading politician of the 460s (*Ath.Pol.* 27.1); Hyperbolus likewise began his career with prosecutions (ARISTOPHANES, *Acharnians* 845-7).

As in most political systems, very few politicians made it to the top, which in Athens meant being the leading member of a political group.

Accountability, risk and reward

Under the democracy supreme power rested with the demos. This power is registered vividly in the dramatic metaphor of Aristophanes' *Knights*, where Demos personified is presented as a householder, with the politicians as his slaves. An important aspect of the exercise of this power was the accountability of public officials: either directly through the Assembly or the courts, or indirectly through the Council, the demos exercised a close scrutiny over its servants. Through the procedures for *dokimasia* on commencement of office, *euthynai* on termination of office, the regular opportunities each prytany for deposition of officials, through the opportunities for political charges through the courts, the demos was able to maintain its control. This control was increased by the fragmentation of administrative power through the use of boards rather than individuals, since, unless all were corrupted together, members of each board could be expected to watch each other.

The punishment for misconduct could be severe. Antiphon, warning the jurors against a hasty decision, reminds them of an occasion when the whole board of the Hellenotamiae were condemned to death:

> Again, your Hellenotamiae, when accused falsely, as I am now, of theft, were put to death out of anger rather than reason, all but one; and the truth was discovered subsequently. This one man – they say his name was Sosias – had been condemned to death but had not yet been executed. Meanwhile it was revealed how the money was lost and the man was set free by your Assembly, though he had already been handed over to the Eleven; but the others had all been killed, though they were completely innocent.
> (ANTIPHON 5.69-70)

Greek orators lie with ease, but a dramatic invention like this could not be sneaked past an audience and so probably he is telling the truth, though he may be embroidering details.

But the risks were unevenly distributed: it was the elected officials who were especially exposed, above all the generals. Operating at long range, they were required to show initiative but, inevitably in so doing they risked incurring the anger of the demos if plans backfired. The demos had high, sometimes unrealistic, expectations of their military commanders and the price for disappointing those expectations could be severe. Pericles was deposed as general in 430, tried and fined, when the lack of success in the war was compounded by the suffering of the plague (THUCYDIDES 2.65.3-4). The generals who returned to Athens from Sicily in 424, having failed to bring off the military success the Athenians expected (because the Sicilians temporarily put aside their differences to deprive Athens of an opportunity to intervene) were tried for corruption and severely punished: two were exiled and one was fined (THUCYDIDES 4.55.3). The generals who failed to pick up the wounded after the battle of Arginusae in 406 were tried all together and those foolish enough to return were executed (XENOPHON, *Hellenica* 1.7.1-34). Though the collective trial was unconstitutional, there is no reason to doubt that the generals would have been severely punished if they had been given a proper trial. We have evidence for a large number of trials of generals during the fourth century, resulting in enormous fines or executions. Timotheus, for instance, who played a major role in the creation of the Second Athenian League, was tried for treason in 356/5 and fined 100 talents (DINARCHUS 1.14, 3.17).

Envoys to other Greek states were also in an exposed position. These too might be called upon to make decisions on their own initiative, for which they might find themselves under attack on their return. The Athenian envoys who went to Macedon in 346 to receive Philip's oath under the Peace of Philocrates found the capital full of envoys from other Greek states. The Third Sacred War was still in progress between the Phocians – who had seized Delphi in 356 – and a number of states, in particular Thebes. Philip was preparing a campaign to settle the war and all the envoys were trying to secure a settlement favourable to their own state. Aeschines wanted the Athenian group to intervene: according to him, Demosthenes was more cautious:

> Philip is setting off to Thermopylae; I cover my eyes. Nobody is going to put me on trial for Philip's military exploits but for any statement I make that I should not or any action beyond my instructions. (AESCHINES 2.107)

Aeschines may misrepresent Demosthenes; but an envoy might well feel vulnerable. Aeschines was charged with corruption for his role in negotiating the peace with Macedon; he was acquitted when he came to trial in 343. But another envoy, Philocrates, the main proponent of the peace, felt that its unpopularity made his conviction a certainty; he fled when impeached by Hyperides and was tried and condemned in his absence. The Athenian envoys who in 392/1 at a conference agreed to peace terms which the Assembly rejected were likewise tried and condemned in absence (DEMOSTHENES 19.277-9).

The severity with which generals and envoys were treated reflects in part the difficulty of democratic control at such distances and the consequent need for deterrence through exemplary punishments. We have excellent anecdotal evidence that the deterrent force was felt by those for whom it was intended in Diodorus' account of the general Chabrias' behaviour at the battle of Naxos in 376. Chabrias broke off his pursuit of the residue of the defeated Spartan fleet to rescue the Athenian wounded, because he remembered the lesson of Arginusae (DIODORUS 15.35).

Though the public speakers were not technically officials, they too were answerable for the advice they gave the Assembly. The risks for public speakers, either from explicitly political trials or from trials where the political agenda lurked behind an ostensibly non-political charge, were considerable. They rarely faced death; as a rule a public speaker who was condemned to death was convicted in another capacity (such as envoy or general), perhaps because it was often difficult to attach a particular setback unambiguously to a single speaker. But enormous fines were common, often on a scale designed to impoverish even a rich man and eradicate him as a political force, or to leave him a debtor to the state and therefore deprived of political rights. While politics is always a tough business, the readiness of politicians bringing prosecutions to demand severe penalties strikes the modern as vindictive. However, this treatment of politics as a process of outright winners and outright losers with little between (a 'zero sum game') was almost inevitable within the structures in operation. In a direct democracy with no formal parties, no procedure existed to give a political group an extended mandate to pursue its policies. A politician could influence policy indefinitely and only extreme measures could be guaranteed to neutralise him.

For much of the fifth century political leaders were subject to the ostracism vote. Unlike political trials, ostracism did not require an allegation of misconduct, merely a commitment from the demos to hold a vote, a quorum of 6,000, and enough anxiety or ill-will toward an individual to ensure him the largest share of the votes. Plutarch's anecdote (*Aristides*

7.7) of Aristides' encounter with the Athenian who asked him to write the name Aristides on the shard 'because I'm tired of hearing him everywhere called "the just"', though suspect, rightly emphasises the absence of the need for any substantive charge. There was a rash of ostracisms in the 480s; from then on they became less frequent. Victims included Themistocles, ostracised in the late 470s, possibly as the result of a struggle between pro- and anti-Spartan elements in Athens. Another was Cimon, ostracised in the late 460s; Cimon had staked his credibility on a policy of firm friendship with Sparta and his expulsion was probably concerted with the reforms of Ephialtes as part of a simultaneous restructuring of internal politics and external realignment with democratic Argos. Thucydides, the son of Melesias, was ostracised in the late 440s, thus leaving Pericles as the dominant figure in Athenian politics. The principle driving the use of ostracism seems to be the need for a firm choice either between individuals or between policies. Though there was a free (any name could be inscribed) and secret vote, political factions worked hard to influence the result. The substantial numbers of shards showing the same name written in a single hand probably indicate not only the existence of a minor service industry in writing names for the illiterate but also the production by political factions of ready-made votes for distribution to those attending. One of the names on these pre-inscribed shards is Hyperbolus, the victim of the last ostracism in or soon after 417, and the evidence of the shards agrees with Plutarch's account of the manoeuvring by the factions of Nicias and Alcibiades against him (*Aristides* 7.5, *Alcibiades* 13, *Nicias* 11). Ostracism fell into disuse after this, though it remained available for use and as late as the 320s the vote was still taken whether to hold an ostracism (*Ath.Pol.* 43.5). According to Plutarch the procedure was abandoned because its use for a contemptible figure like Hyperbolus brought it into disrepute. Plutarch's account draws heavily on the comic depiction of Hyperbolus and on Thucydides' evident contempt for him (8.73.3). In fact, ostracism was a blunt instrument, since it removed discord by depriving the city of a potentially useful individual for ten years. With the availability of more subtle means of control, in particular the *graphe paranomon*, ostracism may simply have seemed rather crude.

Public speakers were also subject to the law governing the procedure of *eisangelia* ('impeachment'), one clause of which classed the taking of bribes by a speaker to misguide the Assembly as treason (HYPERIDES 4.7-8). However, the most common weapon against public speakers was the indictment for illegal proposals, *graphe paranomon* (see pp. 56-7 above). *Graphe paranomon* played a central role in Athenian political rivalries. According to Aeschines (3.194), the politician Aristophon boasted that he had been unsuccessfully prosecuted by *graphe paranomon* 75 times. Aeschines may be exaggerating, and the length of Aristophon's career (he was active in politics for over half a century) probably made him unusual, but even so the figure shows that prosecution by *graphe paranomon* was an occupational hazard for politicians. Though the public speaker was not technically an officer of the state, the activity was not risk free.

Fig 4 Ostraka.

Given the hazards, it may seem surprising that so many members of the elite were eager to compete for the favour of the demos. But if the risks were great, so were the rewards. The material benefits were considerable. Though public speakers were not paid, it was generally supposed that politics was a path to wealth. Old Comedy is full of allegations of corruption against politicians as a class and they themselves freely hurled accusations of taking bribes at each other. Probably politicians did receive large sums in 'gifts' from states and individuals, either for specific favours or merely to secure goodwill. As we have seen, taking bribes to speak against the city's interests was an offence; and this meant that there was always the risk of attack. But the fact that the law on *eisangelia* explicitly limits itself to cases where a speaker accepts money and 'does not give the best advice to the demos' (HYPERIDES 4.8) suggests that Hyperides does not misrepresent the Athenian view when he says:

> You readily allow the generals and the public speakers to receive considerable rewards. They have received this right not from the laws but from your leniency and generosity. You impose just one condition, that the money they receive should be through their influence with you, not against your interests. (5.24-5)

Yet it would be a mistake to focus solely on financial benefits. The Greeks, including the Athenians, remained highly sensitive to issues of honour and dishonour. The successful politician amassed enormous prestige, which could be measured in formal awards (more common in the fourth than in the fifth century) such as crowns, gilded or otherwise, preserved on stone inscriptions that would serve as a permanent record. Such prestige was publicly recognised in less tangible but no less important ways through continuing influence in the Assembly and (as supporting speaker or witness) in the courts. And in a society which always viewed the individual within the family context, this prestige continued to be enjoyed by future generations, as we can see in the tendency of speakers in court to claim credit for the achievements of ancestors.

Chapter 6
Democracy in action IV:
Local government; the demes

The demes were the building blocks of Athenian democracy and central to the identity of an Athenian citizen, whose full title was name, father's name and demotic: 'Demosthenes son of Demosthenes of the deme Paiania' (*Demosthenes Demosthenous Paianieus*). Entitlement to deme membership was based on the place of residence of paternal ancestors at the time of Cleisthenes' reforms. Though there was a strong link between membership and residence, not all members lived in the deme. Hence the speaker of Demosthenes 57, explaining why members slipped away from an extraordinary meeting of the deme Halimous held in Athens, finds it useful to explain:

> I was roughly sixtieth, and I was called last of all those who were called on that day, when the older demesmen had gone off to the country; for since our deme, judges, is thirty-five stades [about 6.5 km] from the city and most members live there, the majority had gone off, and those who remained were no more than thirty. (DEMOSTHENES 57.10)

The demes varied enormously in size, as we can see from the lists of Council members returned from each, from Acharnae which returned 22 members to small villages which returned one or two.

The demes were essential to the functioning of the polis: at the most basic level, it was through deme membership that an Athenian acquired his citizen rights. Only when he had been accepted by his deme and had his name entered on its register could an Athenian exercise the full rights of a citizen. In addition to the regular scrutiny of new members, the demes were used at least twice for a procedure of extraordinary scrutiny (*diapsephis*) during the classical period: the first was in 445/4 after a gift of grain from Egypt (PLUTARCH, *Pericles* 37.3, ARISTOPHANES, *Wasps* 716-8) which was distributed among the citizen population; the second was in 346/5 (DEMOSTHENES 57, AESCHINES 1.77, 86). On each occasion the deme voted on each member in turn. Both scrutinies removed substantial numbers from the deme lists.

The demes also played a part in the filling of some posts in the city administration: Council membership was based not just on tribe but on deme. The demes were also involved in the selection of public arbitrators (see p. 40 above) and at some (unspecified) period had played a role in the pre-selection of candidates for offices selected by lot; but by the 320s this had been abandoned because of problems with corruption (*Ath.Pol.* 62.1).

However, the demes were more than a mechanism to facilitate the central administration. They also had a political life of their own and were important for local government. In many respects their structures and activities, which were put in place by Cleisthenes, mirrored those of the city. As with the city, each deme had its own assembly, called the *agora* (the term *ekklesia* was reserved for the state Assembly on the Pnyx), which met as required. All adult male members of the deme were eligible to attend meetings, which were conducted like the Athenian Assembly, with formal proposals which were then inscribed on stone as deme decrees. Like the decrees of the Athenian Assembly, those of the demes ranged from practical business to formal bestowal of honours. The deme assembly business included the election of local officials, who like state officials were subject to a *dokimasia* before serving (DEMOSTHENES 57.25-6) and *euthynai* on leaving office. Like the state, the demes owned land, which would be leased out. They also had their own cults, for the financing of some aspects of which they imposed liturgies. The financial activity of some demes at least involved the charging of a tax (*enktetikon*) on non-members owning land in the deme.

In one important respect the demes and the city operated as separate spheres. We might expect the aspiring politician to use local government to hone his political and administrative skills, as happens in some modern democracies; but as far as we can tell, individuals who play a prominent part in deme affairs are not prominent in state politics.

The principal official was the demarch (*demarchos*), selected by lot, who combined the modern roles of mayor and chief executive of a borough council. The demarch also had control over the deme register and presided over meetings of the assembly. It was his job to pursue anyone defaulting on rents due to the deme (DEMOSTHENES 57.63). He participated in the organisation of deme cults and in some cases offered sacrifices, in line with the normal convergence between religious and secular activities in Greece. His responsibilities in the area of religion extended to ensuring that those who died in the deme were buried by their relatives, or, if none could be found, contracting out the task on behalf of the deme ([DEMOSTHENES] 43.57-8). He would represent the deme in any court cases (except those arising from appeals against the annual *dokimasia* of new members, when the deme elected five members to act for it, *Ath.Pol.* 42.1).

Though we can construct a model for the broad operation of the demes, in practice they differed significantly in the efficiency with which they conducted their business. The speaker of Demosthenes 57 claims that at one point early in the fourth century the Halimous register was lost and deme members had to reconstruct it by holding a special vote on all their members to check eligibility (DEMOSTHENES 57.26). The speaker is a man with a grudge against his deme, and so we cannot assume that he is telling the truth. But the fact that the allegation could be made suggests that the Athenians themselves accepted that local government in Athens (as in many modern democracies, including Britain) varied enormously in quality. The two state-wide special scrutinies of membership testify to a degree of suspicion about the consistency of administrative standards across the demes. We learn from the entry under *Potamos* in the lexicographer Harpocration that this deme in particular (rightly or wrongly) was notorious for its casual approach to the admission of new members.

Chapter 7
Democracy in action V:
Political space in democratic Athens

We begin our mental tour of democratic Athens in the Agora. In the Bronze Age and through the dark ages following the fall of the Mycenaean palace kingdoms, the area subsequently known as the Agora was used as a burial ground. It was not until the late archaic period that the Agora started to take on its role as the administrative centre of the city of Athens, with the appearance of the first substantial administrative buildings; even then, it was not exclusively administrative. *Agora* means (among other things) 'market'; but the Athenian Agora was not the same as the market. The term was also used to designate a clearly defined area marked out by boundary stones (inscribed 'I am the boundary of the Agora'). The Agora in this narrower sense was sacred, and there were containers of water at certain points for those entering it to cleanse themselves. Some commercial activity went on there, but most of the shops were immediately outside this designated area, spilling out of the large square into the neighbouring streets (there were also shops elsewhere in the city). The administrative buildings within the area can be divided into a number of groups.

On the west side of the square, below the low hill of Colonus on which the temple to Hephaestus stands, about halfway down the west side of the Agora, stood the Council Chamber (*Bouleuterion*). There were actually two Council buildings: little remains of the older Council building, which is commonly dated to about 500, immediately after the reforms of Cleisthenes. It appears to have had an anteroom on the south side with the larger meeting room occupying about two-thirds of the site. This building was superseded in the last two decades of the fifth century by a new Council Chamber, which was built immediately behind it. The Old Bouleuterion was not demolished but served as the sanctuary to the Mother of the Gods, hence its name, the *Metroon* ('mother's shrine'). It was here that in the last decade of the fifth century the Athenians created an archive of legal statutes from the same desire to impose order on the collective body of the laws which led to the redrafting of the code (p. 27 above).

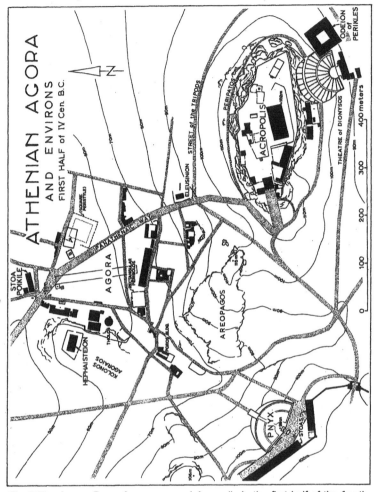

Fig 5 The Agora, Pnyx, Areopagus and Acropolis in the first half of the fourth century.

The Council Chamber, both new and old, had a sacral character. There were divine statues (the later traveller Pausanias mentions statues of Demos, the people personified, Apollo and Zeus Bouliaios – Zeus of the Council). There was also a hearth, which again was sacred. It was here that Theramenes took refuge in 403 when under threat from Critias as the oligarchy of the Thirty fragmented. Theramenes was dragged off by the Scythian archers, in what was for the Greeks a shocking act of sacrilege (XENOPHON, *Hellenica* 2.3.50-56).

In front of the Metroon during the fourth century (earlier their position may have been further south) stood the statues of the eponymous heroes, i.e, the heroes after whom the ten tribes created by Cleisthenes were named. Their location within the Agora probably reflects a desire after

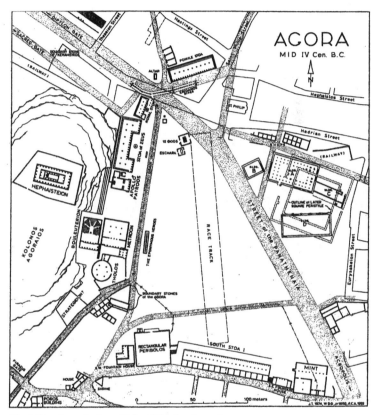

Fig 6 The Agora in the middle of the fourth century.

Cleisthenes' reforms to give prominence to the new tribal system. These statues figure quite prominently in our literary sources. This is not a matter of aesthetics or religion. Rather, it reflects the public role played by the statues in the communications system of ancient Athens: they served as a place for posting public notices. We know for instance that when there was to be a military campaign the names of those required for service were posted by the statues of the eponymous heroes. Aristophanes gives us a vivid account of the individual response to this notice:

> The expedition leaves tomorrow.
> But he hasn't bought his provisions – he didn't know he was going.
> Then standing by the statue of Pandion he sees his name and
> dumbfounded at the disaster he runs off with a look like vinegar.
>
> (*Peace* 1181-4)

The statues were also used for posting notice of lawsuits. Under the fourth-century procedures for legislation, we find provision for draft statutes to be placed for inspection in front of them.

Fig 7 The eponymous heroes (reconstruction).

Immediately to the south of the Old Bouleuterion was a round building known as the Tholos. Its shape is still clearly visible in the Agora excavations. This building served as the headquarters of the Prytaneis, the executive committee of the Council. It was in the Tholos that the Prytaneis used to dine at state expense. Part of their number slept there so that there was always a contingent of the Council on duty in case of emergency (see p. 44 above). Fragments of crockery probably used at the Tholos have been found. These are marked with the letters ΔE (delta epsilon), short for *demosios*, 'public property', to prevent members of the Prytaneis from absent-mindedly taking the crockery home for their personal use.

There are a number of other buildings we need to consider before we leave the Agora. By the end of the fifth century there were a number of porticoes (open-sided structures affording shelter from sun and rain) on the edge of the Agora. On the west side north of the Bouleuterion were the porticoes (stoas) of Zeus Eleutherios (built in the second half of the century) and the Stoa of the Basileus (*Stoa Basileios*). On the north side of the Agora was the Stoa of the Herms and the Stoa Poikile (Painted Portico); there was yet another stoa on the south side of the Agora. One or two of these deserve a little more detail. The Royal Stoa was associated with the official known as the Basileus (King-Archon), one of the nine archons; his functions were largely of a religious nature and included convening trials for homicide (see p. 62 above). We know that this stoa was occasionally used as a venue for the court of the Areopagus. It was in the Stoa of the Basileus that the stone tablets bearing the reinscribed laws were set up at the end of the fifth century.

Fig 8 Shield dedicated after the capture of the Spartans at Pylos.

The other portico worth pausing at is the Painted Portico (*Stoa Poikile*). It was built toward the middle of the fifth century and derived its names from the paintings by celebrated artists which adorned the walls. The pictures had a profoundly political character (in the broadest sense): they celebrated Athenian military achievements, directly or indirectly. One painting depicted Marathon and was matched by pictures of the battle of Theseus against the Amazons and the sack of Troy; this both heroised the Persian Wars and located them in the context of a tradition of east-west hostility. We know that another picture depicted a battle against Sparta. The Athenians also dedicated captured shields here, including those taken from the Spartans at Pylos. One of these survives and is now in the Agora Museum. It reads 'The Athenians from the Spartans from Pylos', i.e. 'the Athenians dedicated this shield out of the spoils from Spartans taken at Pylos' (dedications are commonly abbreviated in this way). The building was also used as a lawcourt.

This brings us to another important aspect of the Agora. So far we have largely been looking at it as an administrative centre, but it was also the focal point for judicial activities. There was no single lawcourt in Athens but many: to run the legal system the city needed a range of buildings of different sizes. We know the names of a number of lawcourts, although it is difficult to identify them with confidence. Part of the problem is that the buildings used as courts were not necessarily distinguished architecturally, while those that were (such as the Stoa Poikile and the Odeum by the Theatre of Dionysos) were not exclusively lawcourts. There was a large building in the south west corner of the Agora which has traditionally been designated 'Heliaia', that is, one of the largest courts; unfortunately recent research suggests that, though it was to some degree connected with legal and administrative activities, it may not have been a court. One can be more confident about the building in the north-east corner, where voting ballots were found of a sort described as used in the fourth century (discs pierced with a short rod, a hollow rod for conviction, a solid rod for acquittal). Two other important pieces of court furniture have been found in the Agora. The first is an allotment machine (*kleroterion*) used in the fourth century to select jurors for the day and allocate them to courts. The second is a water-clock (*klepsydra*), a crude but effective device consisting of a pot with a hole at the base; the hole could be stopped with a bung. The pot was filled with water and when the trial began the bung was removed. The amount of water (and so the number of pots) allowed varied according to the importance of the type of case; when the water ran out the speaker had to stop. Though we can use this device to calculate the time allowed for cases in classical Athens, we do not know for certain that it is identical with the containers used in court, since it is inscribed with the name of the tribe Antiochis, not designated as city property.

If in our minds we leave the Agora by the south-west corner, we come to two adjacent hills which between them map out the constitutional history of fifth-century Athens, the Pnyx and the Areopagus.

The Areopagus site reveals little of its historical importance. The key political site of democratic Athens was the adjacent hill of the Pnyx, the regular site for meetings of the Assembly. Unlike the Areopagus, the Pnyx reveals a lot about its history. Although only citizens could participate, there was space for outsiders to observe proceedings; the audience sat on the ground in a banked auditorium. The speakers addressed them from a raised rostrum (the *bema*). During the fifth century the natural contours of the hill dictated the orientation of the site; the audience faced north and the speakers' platform faced south. Around 400 BC there was

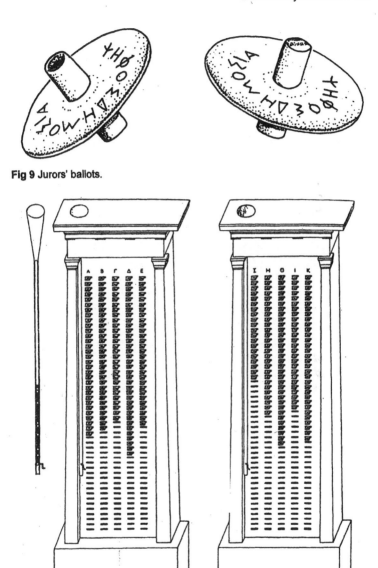

Fig 9 Jurors' ballots.

Fig 10 The *kleroterion* for allocating jurors to courts (reconstruction).

a major reconstruction of the site and the positions were reversed, as we know both from literary and from archaeological evidence. Our literary source (PLUTARCH, *Themistocles* 19.4) ascribes the change to the Thirty and explains it as an ideological move: the speakers' platform was turned from the sea, associated with the navy and democracy, to face the land. A more plausible explanation is that the intention was to shelter the

Fig 11 The *klepsydra* or waterclock (reconstruction). Inscription reads: '(Property) of (the tribe) Antiochis (contents) two choes' (=6.4 litres).

audience from the wind. In fact, from the end of the sixth century Athens had a capacious auditorium with good shelter from the wind, the Theatre of Dionysus on the southern slope of the Acropolis, which would have been an ideal location for the assembly; but this location was rarely used in the classical period. The Assembly regularly met there after the Dionysia in the spring to discuss the conduct of the festival (AESCHINES 2.61, DEMOSTHENES 21.8) and – by the 320s – there was a further meeting at which the ephebes (see p. 40 above) gave a military display (*Ath.Pol.* 42.4). However, the Pnyx was so obviously the proper location for the Assembly that in Aristophanes' *Knights* (42) the personification of the Athenian people, Demos, is given as his deme-title, 'Demos Pyknites', 'Demos of Pnyx.' Possibly, as has been suggested, the reluctance to move is in part due to conservatism, in part to the significance of the position; the hill was close to the Agora, the civic centre of Athens. The conservatism has a religious dimension, since Assembly meetings were religious as well as secular occasions.

Directly east of the Pnyx is the Propylaea, the monumental entrance to the Acropolis. Although (according to Thucydides) the Acropolis had

Fig 12 The speaker's platform (*bema*) on the Pnyx, late fourth century.

once – with the area immediately to the south – been the whole city, it was never in the classical period either inhabited or used as an administrative centre. It was always given over to cult use, so the whole site had to be kept ritually pure. This is best illustrated by two scenes in Aristophanes' *Lysistrata*. When Myrrhine teases her husband with the promise of sex, one ploy to keep him at bay is to ask him how she is to purify herself (912-13). When the women, desperate for sex, try to escape from the Acropolis which they have seized, one of them claims to be pregnant (742-55). Sex and childbirth alike leave the participant ritually unclean. The Acropolis was the end point of the most significant procession in the Athenian calendar, the Panathenaea, itself a profoundly political act (in the widest sense). Members of the whole population (not just the citizen body) took part in the parade, divided into different groups, and the citizen body was also subdivided for the procession. It was a visual definition of the different components yet at the same time a process which united and defined the whole population. The Acropolis was of course the best defensive position in Athens and for this reason (as well as because it contained the treasury of Athena) it is the site seized by the women in Aristophanes' *Lysistrata*, as it had, in reality, been seized by Cylon and his co-conspirators in the late seventh century and by the Spartan forces of Cleomenes in the late sixth century. But beyond its practical political importance, the Acropolis and its buildings had a symbolic political aspect. The orator Aeschines (writing in the middle

Fig 13 The Propylaea seen from the Pnyx.

of the fourth century) gives us an idea of this symbolic value when he talks about the debate which led to the conclusion of peace with Macedon in 346 BC. He represents the speakers who opposed peace as appealing to Athens' great past; but the way they expressed themselves is revealing. According to Aeschines, they urged the Assembly to look to the Propylaea, which all present could see simply by turning their heads and looking due east (2.74). In the same speech Aeschines claims that the Theban general Epameinondas had proposed to set the Athenian Propylaea on the Cadmea, i.e., the Theban citadel (2.105). The claim may be invention, but the symbolism is clear: the Propylaea here stands for Athens' role as one of the dominant cities of Greece.

Tucked into the south-east side of the Acropolis is the theatre of Dionysus. Though Athenian drama never had a formal political role, it was by definition *politikos*, 'of the polis', by its location within the annual state festivals. The dramatic festivals vividly illustrate the convergence of religious and secular in the ancient Greek polis. Their importance can be seen in the introduction during the fourth century of the theoric payments (see p. 39 above) to ensure a large citizen presence. The principal festival for tragedy, the City Dionysia, was held in spring, when there would be a large number of foreigners in Athens. We know (from the fact that Athens was exporting tragedy as early as Aeschylus) that Athenian tragedy was much admired outside Athens. The festival, in particular the theatrical spectacle, was therefore at one level a sustained display of Athenian cultural pre-eminence. The Athenians exploited the foreign presence to make the festival an exercise in propaganda. It was at this time of the year that the members of the Athenian empire would bring the tribute in the fifth century, and we are told that the tribute was displayed in the theatre (ISOCRATES 8.82). Grants of honours to citizens and foreigners were sometimes announced in the theatre; and it was here that the orphans of Athenians killed in war would parade on reaching maturity to receive the blessing of the demos and a gift of armour (AESCHINES 3.154). The festival thus displayed to the Greek world the wealth, power, and prestige of Athens, the public spirit of her citizens, and the readiness of the demos to repay this, as well as the status of Athens as the artistic centre of Greece. The use of the theatre as a show-case survived the loss of the empire: this was not just propaganda for external purposes. All ritual has as its purpose – at one level – the celebration of group identity, and the dramatic festivals, together with the Panathenaic procession in the summer, are an important celebration of Athenian identity. As many scholars have observed, within this context the tragedians respond indirectly to contemporary events, providing another forum for the discussion of issues of concern. Since the capacity of the theatre in the late fifth century was between two and three times that of the Pnyx, a much larger proportion of the population will have been present at the dramatic performances than at the Assembly.

It is comedy however, at least in the fifth and early fourth century, which engages directly with contemporary politics. In general, comedy focuses not on policy but on personalities and style. The prominent political figures are mercilessly satirised, either in passing or as the target of whole plays. Though we tend to see, and admire, Pericles through Thucydides' eyes, we know that he was mocked ceaselessly by the comic poets; and as each of his successors, Cleon, Hyperbolus, Cleophon, became the dominant figure on the Pnyx, he was singled out for lampoon by the comic stage. It is impossible to tell in most cases how far the satire represents the poet's own views; but since the dramatists were in competition for popular favour, the recurrent attacks on leading politicians presumably reflect what the audience enjoyed. We are faced therefore with the paradox that the Athenians simultaneously gave influence and prestige and mocked its recipients. It has been suggested that the audience in the theatre was more wealthy, and more hostile to the demagogues, than the Assembly. The suggestion is based on the cost of attendance, which for a family would be expensive over the several days of the festival before the introduction of theoric payments. But this is to ignore the importance of the festival and therefore the likelihood that people

Fig 14 The theatre of Dionysus.

would save in order to attend, especially as it was only an annual event. There is no objective evidence that the citizens in the theatre audience differed significantly from the Assembly in their attitudes. So the paradox remains. Nowhere is this more visible than in the case of Cleon, who was lampooned by Aristophanes in a play (*Knights*), which won first prize, but who was elected general very shortly afterwards. In part this paradox perhaps reflects the resentment arising within a political system which gave political control to the masses whilst giving political initiative, and substantial rewards, to elite politicians. It also points to a practical purpose served by comedy, which helped to keep politicians in their place by reminding them where power really lies; as such, it supplemented the more formal means of democratic control. This role for comedy as a means of democratic control is recognised by the Old Oligarch:

> They do not allow ridicule and abuse of the demos, to avoid being criticised themselves, but in the case of individuals they encourage anyone who wishes, in the firm knowledge that the

individual ridiculed is not as a rule one of the demos or the mass but someone with wealth or good birth or power. Very few poor people or members of the demos are ridiculed, and these only if they make a nuisance of themselves or seek to have more than the demos. ([XENOPHON] *Ath.Pol.* 2.18)

Though the author oversimplifies (the demos is occasionally a comic target, most notably in Aristophanes' *Knights*), he accurately grasps the relationship between informal and formal control of men of influence by the demos.

Next to the theatre stood the Odeum of Pericles, a large square structure whose roof was supported on pillars. As well as serving as a hall for various purposes, like many large halls in Athens it served as a court room and is attested as such by the 420s.

To the south east of the theatre stood another two buildings which have been identified tentatively with courts: the Palladium and the Delphinium. These were two of the homicide courts. Athenian homicide procedures allocated cases to courts according to factors such as the nature of the charge, the nature of the defence and the status of the victim. The Delphinium was the court used when the accused admitted homicide but claimed the act was justified, while the Palladium tried cases where people were charged with involuntary homicide or causing death through an intermediary, or if the victim was a slave, a metic or a foreigner.

Chapter 8
Democracy and its critics

The past is never transparent; and it is never inert, unless it is very remote indeed. It is endlessly rewritten in the light of contemporary experience and constantly cited for its capacity to influence thinking in the present. The evaluation of Athenian democracy has been particularly prone to fluctuation according to the constitutional context of the researcher. For most readers in the western world at the beginning of the twenty-first century the superiority of democracy over other systems is an uncontested fact; but for eighteenth century writers 'democracy' was not a positive term, and this attitude spilled over into the nineteenth. In a much-quoted statement, the poet Wordsworth observed: 'I am of that odious class of men called democrats'. It was not until the latter part of the nineteenth century that democracy became (in the language of *1066 and all that*) an incontestably Good Thing.

But Athenian democracy was controversial even for its contemporaries. In classical Greece the dominant form of government was aristocracy. Athens was unusual in maintaining democracy almost uninterrupted for the best part of two centuries. Our surviving texts from the period all come from members of the elite, and not surprisingly some are highly critical of democracy.

For some critics the root problem with democracy is the notion of equality. Though the Athenians never adopted the view that all members of society are equal in terms of ability, at heart democracy assumes that collective decisions are more reliable than individual decisions and that all people to some degree are capable of intelligent thought. Yet an Assembly made up of artisans, labourers and traders inevitably aroused a degree of disdain in anyone convinced of the natural right of the aristocrat to rule; this disdain finds expression in the dismissive remarks of Xenophon's Socrates (*Memorabilia* 3.7.5-6) on the membership of the Athenian Assembly. The principle of *isegoria* goes further, since equal access to the rostrum presupposes that the advice of the poor can be as useful as that of the rich and the layman's advice as good as the dedicated politician. Plato's Socrates pokes mischievous fun at the principle that anyone should address the Assembly:

I observe that whenever we gather in the Assembly, when the city must deal with building they send for builders to advise on the buildings, and when it's about the construction of ships, we send for the shipbuilders, and this is the case with everything else which they think can be learned and taught. And if anyone else whom they don't consider a craftsman tries to advise them, even if he's handsome or rich or one of the noble, they still don't tolerate it but laugh and heckle, until the man attempting to speak is forced by the din to step down or the archers drag or carry him off on the orders of the Prytaneis. This is how they act on issues which they think are a matter of skill. But when there is need for a decision on the running of the city, a carpenter will stand up and advise them, a smith or cobbler – it's all the same – a trader or ship's captain, rich or poor, highborn or low, and nobody opposes these as in the cases mentioned before, because, though he has not learned from any source and he has no teacher, he still attempts to offer advice.

(PLATO, *Protagoras* 319c-d)

The Theban herald in Euripides' *Suppliant Women* is equally dismissive:

The poor farmer,
even if he were not ignorant, because of his work
could not turn his gaze to public affairs.
This causes vexation for the better men
when some low man [*poneros*] has prestige
winning over the demos with his tongue, when he was nothing
  before.   (*Suppliant Women* 420-5)

The same prejudice is expressed by the Old Oligarch, who observes ([XENOPHON] *Ath.Pol.* 1.6) that the advantage for the masses is that the speakers have the same (low) aims as themselves and therefore operate to their common advantage. Aristotle is critical of egalitarianism based on number rather than merit (*Politics* 1301a29-40). One of the speakers in Herodotus' fictitious debate on constitutional models observes that the mass is uneducated and unintelligent (3.81.2). Ultimately what we have here is simple class prejudice based on the traditional claim to superiority of those with old money. This was a prejudice daily reinforced by the survival of a vocabulary which identified social status with moral superiority: the wealthy were 'the best men' (*hoi aristoi*) 'the best element' (*to beltiston*) while the word *poneros* could be used to mean 'rogue', 'villain' or by aristocratic writers to designate a man of low socio-economic status. This disdain for the mass was secretly shared by some politicians who achieved eminence under the democracy, to judge by Alcibiades' dismissal of democracy as 'acknowledged folly' in his speech at Sparta in Thucydides 6.89.6 (though he is of course trying to win over a Spartan audience).

Perhaps the best contemporary answer to these prejudices is offered by Thrasybulus in the speech attributed to him by Xenophon in his account of the restoration of the democracy in 403:

> 'My advice to you,' he said, 'men of the city [that is, those who had supported the Thirty, as distinct from the democrats who had seized Piraeius] is to know yourselves. The best way to do this is if you were to reflect why you should feel proud and seek to rule us. Is it because you are more just? But the demos, though more poor than you, has never yet done you wrong for money. But you, who are richer than everyone, have committed many shameful acts for profit. But since you have no claim to justice, ask yourselves if you should be proud of your courage. And what better test of this could there be than the way we warred against each other. But perhaps you could claim that you are superior in judgement; yet despite having city walls and heavy armour and the Peloponnesians for your allies you were deprived by men who had none of these advantages. Or do you think you should be proud because of the Spartans? Why should you, when like men who muzzle and hand over biting dogs they have gone off, having handed you over to the demos here that you have wronged.'   (*Hellenica* 2.4.40-41)

Critics also associate democracy with indiscipline. The freedom (*eleutheria*) on which the Athenians prided themselves is for Plato the root cause of the destruction of democracy (*Republic* 562-3), as it degenerates into total indiscipline, though the democratic society Plato depicts (in which fathers fear children, teachers fear pupils, and the laws are held in contempt) is a grotesque parody of democratic Athens. The indiscipline at the heart of democracy is also emphasised by the Old Oligarch:

> Throughout the world the best element [*to beltiston*] is hostile to democracy. For among the best there is least indiscipline and injustice and the most scrupulous commitment to good conduct, while in the demos there is the most disorder and lack of scruple [*poneria*].   ([XENOPHON] *Ath.Pol.* 1.5)

Although rich in irony in view of the contempt of the Athenian oligarchs for law and morality, this is a view shared by other critics of democracy. It is found in Isocrates' complaint (7.20) that the Athenian constitution in his day (the first half of the fourth century) confused lawlessness (*paranomia*) with freedom (*eleutheria*). The idea is already present in Herodotus' debate on the three forms of government – democracy, oligarchy, monarchy – where the unruly passion of the mob is compared to a winter torrent (3.81.2). The same idea lurks behind Thucydides' criticism of the Athenians for fickleness in first deposing and fining and then reinstating Pericles as general early in the Peloponnesian War (2.65.3-4). For Plato this lack of discipline is particularly manifested in the conduct of the Assembly and the courts, where instead of listening in disciplined silence the crowds interrupt noisily. This notion is already present in Pindar's dismissal (*Pythian* 2.87) of the demos as *ho labros stratos*, 'the raucous crowd'. It is picked up in republican Rome by Cicero (*Pro Flacco* 16): 'And so, to leave aside the present Greece which has long been battered and afflicted by its own bad judgement, that Greece of old, which once flourished in wealth, power and renown, fell because of this one thing, the immoderate freedom (*libertas*) and indiscipline (*licentia*) of its assemblies'.

Again, however, there is little in the contemporary criticism beyond the disgruntlement of the aristocrat at the lack of an exclusive right to power and the absence of a culture of automatic deference to status and authority. The Assembly could lose its head, and the Athenians knew it, as they showed when they reopened the debate on Mytilene in 427 after voting to massacre the grown men and enslave the rest of the population. Yet we have seen that Assembly meetings, though lively, were orderly, remarkably so, given their scale. It is important to bear in mind that the critics of democracy will rarely, if ever, have witnessed a political debate in a non-democratic state; they are comparing the Athenian reality with an abstract ideal, an error repeated by many moderns. Thucydides' account of the debate at Sparta which led to the Peloponnesian War (1.79-86) is proof that fierce debate was a feature of Greek, not just democratic, politics.

Plato sees democracy as a constitution which breeds not just unruly but also violent passions. But speakers addressing Assembly or court are as prone to criticise the Athenians for being too soft-hearted. Since the context is often an argument for severity, we cannot be too trusting, but the picture is reproduced in *Ath.Pol.* – of the expulsion of the tyrants, the author notes (22.4): 'The Athenians allowed all the friends of the tyrants who were not implicated in wrongdoing during the disturbances to live in the city, with the usual leniency of the demos'. The demos showed the same generosity after the Thirty in declaring an amnesty. Plato notes in his *Seventh Letter* that the returning democrats behaved with great 'decency'/'moderation' (*epieikeia*), while the *Ath.Pol.*, commenting on the amnesty and the decision of the democrats to repay as the city's debt the money the Thirty had borrowed from Sparta to sustain their regime, observes (40.2): 'I think that of all men they responded to the preceding disasters in the most honourable and public-spirited (*politikotata*) manner, both individually and collectively.'

More serious is the accusation that the Assembly was too easily swayed by skilful speakers. It is here that Thucydides locates the flaws in post-Periclean democracy. For Thucydides democracy required strong leaders; the masses needed to be restrained and the great strength of Pericles was his ability to control the Assembly through his remarkable personal authority. Pericles' successors were all competing on an equal footing and in their struggle for dominance were inclined to give the masses their own way (2.65.10). There is much that is inaccurate in all of this. It is important to note that some ancient commentators made not Cleon but Pericles the first of the demagogues and interpreted some at least of his democratic measures as an attempt to curry favour with the demos; the narrative of decline and fall could be written in more than one way. The picture of Pericles' successors as motivated solely by ambition is heavily influenced by Thucydides' own disappointment at the way in which (as he saw it) the successes of the decades of expansion were squandered.

But Thucydides is not alone in arguing that the democratic Assembly is too easily seduced by a clever speaker. This danger is identified by the Theban herald in Euripides' *Suppliant Women* and again by the messenger in Euripides' *Orestes*. Though the former is an unsympathetic figure, the latter is more difficult to dismiss and it seems that the Athenians themselves identified this as a risk attached to collective decision-making. The danger is inevitable wherever policy is shaped by open debate rather than by fiat or by cabal (though experience also shows that the absence of such debate does not so much prevent haste and error as facilitate concealment). The Athenian answer was to make the public speaker answerable for his proposals. Of course, the demos was not answerable for its response, and speakers occasionally comment on the fact that the speakers are held responsible for collective decisions (THUCYDIDES 2.60.4, 3.43.4). The complaint has some force; but those voting at the Assembly did not escape scot-free, since collectively they felt the impact of policy errors and in military matters could pay with their lives.

Modern critics of Athenian democracy have often echoed the hostility of Athenian writers to the radical democracy, not surprisingly, since academics themselves have traditionally come from, or else joined, the modern elite. But there is another, and opposing strand, which emphasizes the lack, not the excess, of democracy in Athens. Athens never extended political rights to women, resident aliens or slaves. This was explicitly and irrevocably a democracy of adult Athenian males. It is, however, important to bear in mind that the granting of political rights to women is a very recent phenomenon, for most societies a product of the twentieth century. In Britain at least women owe their political rights as much to world war as to enlightened policy. The exclusion of foreigners from political rights is the norm in modern systems, which differ only in their greater readiness to allow outsiders to acquire citizenship. It is probably the exclusion of slaves, as possessions, from almost all rights which particularly offends the modern reader, though for most of the Founding Fathers of the USA it was perfectly compatible with democracy. Here Athens was no better and no worse than any other Greek state of its day, and most subsequent states until the nineteenth century. The defects of the Athenian system, measured against modern ideals, are too obvious to ignore; but compared with most subsequent political systems Athens was remarkably egalitarian.

Another factor which has suggested a democratic deficit in Athens is the role of the elite. The players on the political field were almost always wealthy men and the majority acted as referees, not strikers. Here is Demosthenes' memorable account of the Assembly meeting after Philip's seizure of Elatea in 338:

> Next day at dawn the Prytaneis called the Council to the Council chamber and you made your way to the Assembly, and before the Council had completed its business and drafted its proposals, the whole people was seated up on the hill. Then when the Council had arrived and the Prytaneis had announced the news they had received and brought up the messenger and he had spoken, the herald asked: 'who wishes to speak?' Nobody came forward. Though he repeated the question many times, still nobody stood up....   (DEMOSTHENES 18.169-70)

Demosthenes is describing an emergency so startling that the regular speakers are silent. But in one respect the meeting was typical, in that most ordinary Athenians would never address the Assembly; their response to the herald's invitation was always to remain in their seats. The elite changed in composition during the classical period, with wealth replacing a combination of wealth and birth as the qualification for membership. But whatever its composition, there was always an elite, and in this respect again Athens was not unusual. It is difficult to identify a contemporary developed society which does not have an elite. The Athenians were pragmatic enough to accept this; their aim was not to remove the elite but to ensure that the last word in policy went to the demos, and that politicians were always subject to popular scrutiny and control.

Finally, many moderns have questioned the accuracy of the democratic mantra 'live as one pleases', and more generally whether the Athenians had any conception of individual rights. Certainly the terminology is lacking. The Athenians had a term for positive political rights, though the language used was of 'privilege'/'honour' (*time*) rather than 'right'. But they had no term for individual 'rights' in the modern sense. However, the broader term of *eleutheria* included non-interference by the polis in individual activity which neither threatened the polis nor harmed others. The system did of course produce abuses. Although its fatal outcome was more the result of his intransigence than any fundamental flaw in the legal system, it is almost certain that Socrates' conviction was motivated by residual resentment against the Thirty. His conviction was at least the result of due legal process. But law could be brushed aside in extreme circumstances, as when the generals were tried all together after Arginusae in contravention of a basic legal principle. These are exceptions however, and there is scarcely a democracy in existence where the same tale could not be told.

Ultimately the test of a constitution must be its success in serving the needs of its population. For virtually two centuries Athens enjoyed almost uninterrupted internal stability. Political rivalry, though fierce and not infrequently devastating for politicians and generals, was conducted through constitutional means and according to law. Tension between rich and poor was contained. The rich were compelled to contribute to the state, but there was never (under the democracy) any attempt to strip them of their wealth. Though a wide gulf separated the rich from the poor, attempts were made to protect the most vulnerable members of society. From a utilitarian perspective – the greatest good for the greatest number of people – the Athenian constitution could be judged a success.

During the same period Athens was one of the foremost powers in Greece. For most of the fifth century Athens was the largest and wealthiest, and arguably the most powerful, state on the peninsula. Stripped of empire, walls and ships at the end of the fifth century and reduced to the role of a Spartan vassal, it had recovered sufficient strength within a decade to play a major role in Greek politics, which it did for most of the fourth century. The picture is of course not one of undiluted success. Athens lost the Peloponnesian War and with hindsight one can see mistakes which could have been avoided. But the defeat was as much the result of Spartan access to Persian gold as of Athenian errors. Athens won and lost an empire; but the Spartan supremacy which followed was much shorter (only two decades) and far more oppressive. Ultimately Athens was no match for Macedon, with its vast mineral wealth, its concentration of power in the person of the king, and (crucially) the succession of two quite remarkable rulers, Philip and Alexander. Nor was any other Greek state, irrespective of its constitution.

There is of course more to success than power. During the lifetime of the democracy Athens set the cultural agenda for Greece. In the fifth century, though many of the leading intellectuals were of non-Athenian origin, it was Athens in particular where they found an environment congenial to their activity. The move from physical speculation to ethics as the essence of philosophy (an agenda which has survived to the present day) took place at Athens. Historiography, though originating in Ionia, became quintessentially Athenian. The successor to Herodotus of Hali-carnassus was the Athenian Thucydides. Though Greek prose originated primarily in Ionia, by the end of the fifth century Attic Greek had become the language of prose writing. Hence Gorgias of Leontini in Sicily chooses to write in Attic Greek, not in Ionian or in his native Doric dialect. Pericles' vision of Athens as the school of Hellas is reflected in the export of Athenian tragedy to other parts of the Greek peninsula. In the fourth century Athenian comedy becomes international, and Athens attracts comic writers from other parts of Greece. All this is no mean achievement.

Suggestions for Further Study

1. Is *demokratia* 'democracy'? What are the essential features of democracy for us and how do our expectations compare with Athenian *demokratia*? When we write the history of Athenian democracy, is cultural change as important as constitutional change? Of the phases in the evolution of democracy outlined in this book, which brought the most significant change? Take any one of the sources for reconstructing Athenian democracy (or Athenian views on democracy) and assess its value as evidence. What are the strengths and weaknesses of *Ath.Pol.* as a basis for reconstructing Athenian democracy?

2. What was the nature of the crisis Solon sought to resolve? Was he trying to reform or preserve the existing regime? What groups or sections of society would you expect to support Solon and why? Can we place any trust in our sources on Solon, given that they drew heavily on his poetry? What conclusions about political developments at Athens can we legitimately draw from Solon's own statements?

3. How did the tyranny of Peisistratus and his sons contribute to the political development of Athens? How important was the tyranny as an influence on Cleisthenes' reforms?

4. Did Cleisthenes have a political programme or was he an opportunist? If he had a political programme, what do you suppose it to be? How seriously should we take Herodotus' description of Athens after Cleisthenes as a *demokratia*? Would Aristotle have recognised it as such? If it was a *demokratia*, what was it about Cleisthenes' reforms that made it so?

5. If Cleisthenes created ostracism, why was it unused for 20 years? Why was it brought into use in the 480s? For what purposes was ostracism used during the course of its existence?

6. Were Ephialtes' reforms as significant as those of Cleisthenes or were they merely the inevitable result of developments in Athens in the first few decades of the fifth century? What does the *Eumenides* of Aeschylus tell us about the reforms of Ephialtes? Where (if anywhere) does Aeschylus stand in the constitutional debate?

7. How important was the empire for the creation and preservation of democracy? In Thucydides, Pericles and others describe the Athenian empire as a *tyrannis*; is there a paradox in a political system based on an ideology of freedom at the apex of an empire? Did Athens export democracy to the empire?

8. Why was there so little active opposition to democracy in Athens? Given the financial burdens, why did wealthy Athenians accept the democracy? What advantages did the wealthy enjoy under the democracy? What if anything did the rich get out of the liturgy system?

9. How democratic was democratic Athens? What role could the ordinary Athenian play in the political processes? Was the Assembly merely a forum for elite competition? Did the Council really run Athens?

10. How real was democratic freedom? Pericles portrays Athens as a tolerant society. Is this (as has been suggested) a whitewash? Did the prosecution system, with its reliance on the volunteer, encourage wholesale interference in the lives of others? Can we harmonise the talk of democratic freedom with the series of prosecutions for impiety in the late fifth century?

11. How important was civic cult to the democracy? In what ways did religion help to define and reinforce the political system?

12. Why do we find a divorce between military command and political influence in the late fifth century? How complete is the divorce? Thucydides perceived a decline in the quality of political leadership after Pericles; how far was he correct? Thucydides describes the difference between Pericles and his successors (in part) in terms of active/passive or controller/controlled. Is this accurate? How (apart from social class) does Cleon differ from Pericles?

13. Was democratic Athens ruthless in its treatment of political leaders? Did the mechanisms for political accountability strengthen or weaken Athens? Was the political role played by the courts a good or a bad thing?

Aristophanes often represents politicians and officials as corrupt; how much room was there for political and administrative corruption in democratic Athens?

14. Did the rules for non-repetition of office and the use of boards of magistrates (rather than individuals) impair the operation of the Athenian state? How was continuity maintained? What, if any, are the advantages of the system?

15. If (like Rip Van Winkel) Pericles were somehow revived in the Athens of Demosthenes, what changes (if any) would he notice? The fourth-century democracy has been described as more conservative than the fifth; is this accurate? Given the change in procedures for legislation in the fourth century and the transfer of impeachment (*eisangelia*) hearings from Assembly to lawcourts in the middle of the century, was the Assembly still sovereign?

Suggestions for Further Reading

Sources

All classical authors quoted are translated by me. Few of the literary sources require explanation. Solon is cited according to the numbering of the second edition of the large Oxford text of Martin West (*Iambi et elegi Graeci*). Fragments of the historians are cited according to the numbering of the majestic but impenetrable multi-volume edition of Felix Jacoby, *Die Fragmente der griechischen Historiker* (Berlin/Leiden 1923-58). Inscriptions wherever possible are cited from R. Meiggs and D.M. Lewis, *A selection of Greek historical inscriptions to the end of the fifth century* (Oxford 1969, repr. 1988) or from P. Harding, *From the end of the Peloponnesian War to the battle of Ipsus* (Cambridge 1985), less frequently from the monumental *Inscriptiones Graecae* (Berlin 1873-). The general reader wishing to access the *Ath.Pol.* could not do better than to acquire the Penguin translation of P.J. Rhodes, *Aristotle: the Athenian Constitution* (Harmondsworth 1984). Rhodes has also produced a weighty commentary on the *Ath.Pol.*, *A commentary on the Aristotelian Athenaion Politeia* (Oxford 1981).

General

The range of books which offer a historical setting for the study of Athenian democracy include:
S. Hornblower, *The Greek world 479-323* (London revised ed., 1991).
R. Sealey, *A history of the Greek city states 700-338 B.C.* (Berkeley and Los Angeles 1976).
    There are a number of accounts of the evolution of the Athenian democracy or of its operation.
    R. Barrow, *Athenian democracy* (ed.2 London 1999) offers an account of the development of the democracy and of its operation in the fifth century. J.K. Davies, *Democracy and classical Greece* (ed.2 Cambridge MA 1993) offers an illuminating and suggestive narrative, with copious but deft use of sources. W.G. Forrest, *The emergence of Greek democracy* (London 1966) traces its theme as far as the emergence of the radical democracy. M.H. Hansen, *The Athenian democracy in the age of Demosthenes*

(second edition, London 1999), focuses on the fourth-century democracy but also offers an account of the evolution of the system; it is learned, informative and readable. C. Hignett, *A history of the Athenian constitution* (Oxford 1952), despite its age, remains a thoughtful and provocative account of the political development of Athens to the end of the fifth century. A.H.M. Jones, *Athenian democracy* (Oxford 1957) provides a general overview of the operation of the democracy which despite its age is still useful. R.K. Sinclair, *Democracy and participation in Athens* (Cambridge 1988) provides a wide-ranging account of the operation of the democracy, with particular emphasis on the extent and nature of citizen participation in politics. D. Stockton, *The classical Athenian democracy* (Oxford 1990) combines an evolutionary account with a description of the operation in the fifth century. J. Thorley, *Athenian democracy* (London 1996) covers the same period.

The democracy is explored from a variety of angles in *Ritual, finance, politics: Athenian democratic accounts presented to David Lewis* (Oxford 1994), edited by Robin Osborne and Simon Hornblower.

Political bodies

The following studies will allow readers to explore specific bodies in the democracy in greater detail:

Assembly: M.H. Hansen, *The Athenian Assembly in the age of Demosthenes* (Oxford 1987). Less easily acquired but invaluable on many matters of detail is his two volume collection of published articles, *The Athenian Ecclesia* (Copenhagen 1983, 1989).

Council: P.J. Rhodes, *The Athenian Boule* (Oxford 1972).

Areopagus: R.W. Wallace, *The Areopagos Council to 307 B.C.* (Baltimore and London 1989); this detailed study offers an alternative on many points to the account offered in this volume.

The courts: D.M. MacDowell, *The law in classical Athens* (London 1978), R.A. Bauman, *Political trials in ancient Greece* (London and New York 1990).

The demes: R. Osborne, *Demos, the discovery of classical Attika* (Cambridge 1985), covers aspects of the demography, sociology, economics and politics of the demes. D. Whitehead, *The demes of Attika 508/7-c.250 BC* (Princeton NJ 1986), provides the most thorough study available of the demes.

Politicians and officials

B.S. Strauss, *Athens after the Peloponnesian War* (New York 1986), though focused on the period after the Athenian defeat, has valuable insights on the operation of political groups. W.R. Connor, *The new politicians of fifth century Athens* (ed.2 Princeton NJ 1971, repr. Indianapolis 1992) is still the most thorough treatment of the type of politician which emerged in the late fifth century. J.T. Roberts, *Accountability in Athenian government* (Madison WI 1982) addresses the central principle of the accountability of officials and politicians.

The elite

The role of the elite in democratic Athens is studied by J. Ober, *Mass and elite in democratic Athens* (Princeton NJ 1989), and J.K. Davies, *Wealth and the power of wealth in classical Athens* (New York 1981).

The empire

R. Meiggs, *The Athenian empire* (Oxford 1972) and P.J. Rhodes, *The Athenian empire, Greece and Rome New Surveys in the Classics* 17 (Oxford 1985) both treat the Athenian empire, the former in detail and at length, the latter in a brief treatment more accessible to the general reader.

The monuments

J.M. Camp, *The Athenian Agora* (London 1986, repr. 1992) deals with the administrative heart of Athens. J. Travlos, *Pictorial dictionary of ancient Athens* (New York 1971) is a rich source of information and images. R.E. Wycherley, *The stones of Athens* (Princeton NJ 1978) offers an excellent general introduction to the ancient city, organised by area.

Ideology and criticism

M.H. Hansen, *Was Athens a democracy? Popular rule, liberty and equality in ancient and modern political thought* (Copenhagen 1989) condenses a wealth of material into a short space. J. Ober and C. Hedrick (ed.), *Demokratia: a conversation on democracies, ancient and modern* (Princeton NJ 1996), assemble a wide-ranging collection of essays by a number of eminent scholars. J. Ober *Political dissent in democratic Athens* (Princeton NJ 1998) discusses the criticism of democracy by Athenian writers. A.W. Saxonhouse, *Athenian democracy: modern mythmakers and ancient theorists* (Notre Dame and London 1996) offers a survey in chapter 1 of the myths woven around Athens by modern scholars.

Religion

Beyond a few throwaway remarks I have said little about religion. J.M. Bremmer, *Greek religion, Greece and Rome New Surveys in the Classics* 24

(Oxford 1994), provides a brief but valuable introduction. R. Parker, *Athenian religion: a history* (Oxford 1996), offers a detailed treatment of Athenian religion. L.B. Zaidman and P. Schmitt Pantel, *Religion in the ancient Greek city* (Cambridge 1992) give a broad account of religion in its civic context. Bauman (above) deals with politically motivated trials for impiety.

Theatre

The political dimension of Athenian theatre has attracted renewed interest in the recent past. This forms the subject of valuable essays on tragedy and comedy by S. Goldhill and J. Henderson in the collection of essays assembled by J.J. Winkler & Froma Zeitlin *Nothing to Do with Dionysus?* (Princeton NJ 1990) and is also discussed by C. Carey. 'Comic ridicule and democracy' in *Ritual, finance, politics*, cited above. For comedy K.J. Dover, *Aristophanic comedy* (Berkeley and Los Angeles 1972) is still useful. For a more wide ranging discussion of the role of performance in Athenian democracy, see *Performance culture and Athenian democracy*, ed. Simon Goldhill and Robin Osborne (Cambridge 1999). See also P.A. Cartledge, 'Deep plays: theatre as process in Athenian civic life' in P.E. Easterling (ed.) *The Cambridge Companion to Greek Tragedy* (Cambridge 1997).

Glossary

Agora: area to the north of the Acropolis, which served as the administrative centre of the city, and also as a marketplace. The term *agora* is also used for the meetings of the deme assemblies (contrast *Ekklesia*).

arche: 'office', a term used both for individual officials and for boards.

Archon: literally 'ruler', the term can refer to any official, but usually (in the plural) it refers to a specific group of nine prestigious public officials, comprising the *Archon basileus*, the *Archon*, the *Polemarchos* and the six *Thesmothetai*.

Archon basileus: 'King Archon', one of the nine Archons, with primarily religious duties.

Areopagus: in full 'The Council of the Areopagus' (*he Boule he ex Areiou pagou*), named from the hill ('the Hill of Ares') west of the Acropolis where it met.

atimia: loss of citizen rights (lit. 'loss of honour/privilege').

Boule: ('Council') the board of 500 which acted as steering group for the *Ekklesia*. The term is also used for the Areopagus, though usually only where the context precludes ambiguity.

choregia: public duty of chorus-producer at a festival; see *leitourgia*.

demagogos: a term for people politically active in the Assembly, anglicised as 'demagogue'.

demarchos: the chief official of the deme ('demarch'); see also *demos*.

demos: according to context the people as a whole or the masses. Inscriptions use the word *demos* to designate the popular Assembly (*Ekklesia*). Demos ('deme') is also the term for the local units (urban sections or villages) which were the smallest political divisions of the democracy.

dikastai: the jurors empanelled in the people's courts (*dikasteria*).

dokimasia: a formal assessment of eligibility for: i) rights; ii) office or activity; iii) benefits.

eisangelia: ('denunciation') a charge for political offences, laid before the Council or the Assembly.

eisphora: levy on assets of the wealthy in times of war.

Ekklesia: the formal meeting of adult male citizens, normally rendered 'Assembly' in English.

ephebeia: ('cadetship') a period of two years' military service performed by citizens immediately on reaching the age of majority.

euthynai: the formal examination of an official on termination of office.

genos: (plural *gene*) 'clan', a kinship group larger than the *oikos*, claiming descent from a shared ancestor.

graphe: the most common public prosecution (often used as a generic term for public prosecutions), open to anyone (*ho boulomenos*), unlike the private prosecution (*dike*), where only the victim could sue.

graphe nomon me epitedeion theinai: public prosecution (fourth century) for laws which contravened existing legislation or were (arguably) against the public interest.

graphe paranomon: public prosecution against any proposal (fifth century), then (fourth century) against decrees only, which contravened existing legislation.

ho boulomenos: generic term for the individual exercising his rights under the democracy either to prosecute in public cases or (less often) to address the Assembly.

leitourgia: ('liturgy') public duties (usually expensive) allocated to the wealthy on the basis of assets.

lexiarchikon grammateion: deme register of its members.

merismos: annual allocation of (their proportion of) state funds to officials in the fourth century.

metoikos: ('metic') an alien resident in Attica; the residency tax he paid was called *metoikion*.

nomothetai: ('lawgivers') panels used to scrutinise new legislation proposed and old legislation subject to repeal in the fourth century.

oikos: the family unit, the smallest kinship/social group.

ostrakismos: Assembly vote under which the individual receiving the largest share of the votes was exiled for ten years, obsolete by the end of the fifth century.

phratria: kinship group larger than the *genos*, claiming descent from a shared ancestor.

Polemarchos: ('Polemarch') one of the nine Archons, with duties especially in relation to resident aliens.

probouleuma: preliminary motion placed before the Assembly by the Council.

proedroi: nine officials, members of Council, who presided over Assembly meetings in the fourth century.

prostates tou demou: 'champion of the *demos*', term for prominent politician.

prytaneia: ('prytany') period of one tenth of the Athenian administrative year, designated from the term of office of the *prytaneis*.

prytaneis: the standing committee of the Council, comprising the full contingent for one of the ten tribes, serving in rotation.

rhetor: 'public speaker', term used from the late fifth century for an active politician.

strategos: 'general', one of a board of ten military officials created by Cleisthenes; in the fifth century these were the most important public officials.

theorika: the money doled out from the *theorikon*.

theorikon: a state fund (the 'Theoric Fund') initiated to provide a dole for theatre attendance, subsequently extended to other types of festival and to building projects.

Thesmothetai: ('Thesmothetae') the title of six of the nine Archons; see also *Archon*.

trierarchia: ('trierarchy') duty of responsibility for equipping and maintaining a trireme; see *leitourgia*.

Index